Cavachons.

The Complete Owner's Manual to Cavachon dogs.

Cavachons care, costs, feeding, grooming, health and training all included.

by

Elliott Lang

Table of Contents

Table of Contents

Table of Contents

Table of Contents

Table of Contents

Introduction

Getting a dog is a huge decision. Your dog will be your faithful companion for anything from 8 to 20 years, based on the breed you chose and their general health. For the adorable Cavachon, you'll be looking at a big commitment as they are smaller dogs and can live for anything from nine to fifteen years, but most live for about twelve years. Over those years it will be your responsibility to care for and protect them from all manner of illnesses, dangers and injuries. You will have to make sure that they feel happy and safe. Dog owners say that about 3-4 hours of their day is taken up with dog-related activities, and that doesn't include spending time with the dog in the evenings watching T.V.

The breed of dog you choose will depend on the lifestyle you intend to build around your dog. If you've owned dogs before then you know how much of a commitment they are, if you haven't then a dog will change your life. Each breed of dog requires different types of care and training, and while their personalities are unique and individual, there are personality traits that are generally accepted to be of the breed. A friend of mine who was a police dog handler always had Alsatians, for example, and these were always big, gentle, well trained animals. He and his wife recently got a little boarder terrier who they say is un-trainable and naughty but so much more fun than their good dogs were.

Chapter 1) Cavachon dogs

1. What are Cavachons?

The Cavachon breed or cross is a great, family friendly indoor dog with bags of personality and relatively few breed-related health problems. They are an active breed that needs a lot of exercise and play. They are also very social animals and will actively seek out people and other dogs to talk to and play with.

Often described as a "designer dog", the Cavachon is a crossbreed. A lot of people will refer to your Cavachon as a mutt. This isn't really an insult and you should try not to be offended by this description – a mutt is a crossbreed. They have all the advantages of a mutt without the uncertainty of size, shape and longevity. They are a cross between the sweet and regal King Charles Clavier, with its beautiful markings and long fur, and the cute, white, fluffy Bichon Fries. The cross here can be any of the colours associated with the King Charles Clavier – black, sable, tan, red, blond and white in all sorts of stunning combinations – though they are generally very pale, which comes from the Bichon Fries. The markings will be the beautiful symmetrical markings seen on the King Charles Clavier. They have big, dark, loving eyes set in their pale faces. They grow to about a foot in height at the shoulders and maintain a good, stocky, youthful shape well into adulthood, weighing 14-20lbs. The fur will be thick and curly, and softer than you would normally expect from a curly haired dog. It stays fluffy like puppy fur, as it gets the softness from both breeds. As the Cavachon comes from two traditional working dogs, they are very bright and are trained very easily with the correct training.

2. Cavachons as pets

Cavachons are sweet, good-natured dogs that get on well with older children and careful younger children.

Because Cavachons are a cross breed – King Charles Cavalier and Bichon Fries – they are far less prone to genetic problems and have a wider gene pool. This results in better breeding practices and healthier dogs in general, though some crosses (pug and Chihuahua springs to mind) can get the worst points of both. The Cavachon has been carefully selected from 2 dogs with good behavioural and health traits, and crossing them was not just an aesthetic decision, even though they are ridiculously cute!

Is this the pet for you?

With a lifespan of 8 to 14 years, a Cavachon is a real commitment. The decision not to get a dog is just as important as the decision to get one and it does not reflect negatively on you if, once everything is considered, you decide you just don't have the time, emotional capacity or resources to be able to give your pooch everything they need. It is a very important decision and you need to make sure that everyone in your house is ready for the new arrival.

3. Questions

There are a number of important questions to ask yourself before you go any further:

Can you afford it?

These dogs are typical of small dogs in that they don't eat as much as larger dogs, but other costs will be the same, and as little dogs they will live longer than larger breeds, so it's a longer term commitment.

Will you be able to make yourself clean up after them?

You are legally obliged to clean up the mess. You can be fined for not cleaning up after a dog has fouled.

Do you have the space?

While Cavachons aren't big dogs, they do need room not to be under your feet all the time. While they don't need as big a house as a Great Dane or a Mastiff, they do need to be able to get about and to get out of your personal space.

Will you be able to play with them as much as they need?

They are energetic, excitable little things and can develop real behavioural problems if they don't get the stimulation they need. Those horrid, yappy little things you see on the street are generally just bored. Cavachons are intelligent and bred from working, thinking dogs.

Can you meet their dietary commitments?

They need regular feeding and constant access to water. If you don't always get to the shops, you need to make sure you have more than enough food to last you to your next shopping visits. It is illegal not to provide adequate food and water.

What would you do if they bite you?

There might be a time when your dog bites you. It may only be a little nip but it needs dealing with. If your dog bites you it's probably your fault, but the consequences for a dog that bites can be awful. If a dog bites you once and you surrender, you can end up with a dangerous dog that you can't handle. Dogs with a bite history are usually put down rather than re-homed.

Do you have the time to properly train your dog?

You need to train your dog. This can take time and energy that some people don't have. You may have an idea that such little dogs don't really need training. Well they do. It's good for you and it's good for them. Even little, sweet Cavachons can be an absolute nightmare when they aren't well trained. A dog that is well trained and knows where it stands is a happy, mentally healthy dog. The training section in this book is extensive.

Can you make the up to 14-year commitment?

The average Cavachon means 14 years of worrying about what to do about holidays, 14 years of insurance, 14 years of keeping on top of behaviour, 14 years of feed, 14 years of hair appointments and the occasional chewed shoe and avoiding people who are afraid of dogs.

What will you do with them when you go away?

Dogs need to be fed and walked while you're on holiday. That is the minimum they need. If you have a dog loving neighbour or friend who will pop in for a few hours to feed and walk and fuss your dog, that would be the ideal situation. There are also kennels that will be very good for your dog, but you need to know what is going to happen to your dog while you are away. If you leave your dog unattended for more than 24 hours you are breaking the law.

4. Costs

You can buy Cavachon puppies for between £200-£500 in the UK and between $500 and $900 in the USA.

If you get an adult or a rescue you'll be looking at £100 or $200 as a re-homing fee.

Castration in the UK will cost £230 -£300 and in the USA it will cost $400 - $600. This one-off fee can save you massive costs in the long run.

Spaying is generally cheaper than castration and can save you huge sums of money as your dog gets older. This will cost £80 to £160 in the UK or $120-$200 in the USA.

Another important one-off cost, though one a lot of people think is not necessary, is micro chipping. Micro chipping only costs about £30 or $60 and can lead to a long-term saving of the total outlay of your dog – it means that if your beloved pooch is missing and found and scanned you will get them back. It means that if they are old or injured and missing and found they won't be put down as an injured stray.

Feed costs can be between £30 and £60 per month or $40 -$70.

Inoculations can cost anything from £30 or $50 a year to £50 or $90 a year and are an absolute must.

Worming will cost £5 or $9 every 2 months. The importance of worming your dog will be discussed later, but this isn't a place to consider making any savings in the upkeep of your dog.

Flea prevention will cost £5 or $8 a month but saves you a lorry load of trouble and expense in the long run.

Insurance will cost about £25 or $50 a month (less when they're puppies, more when they're older)

As Cavachon dogs have relatively long, smooth hair, they will need regular grooming, and you should aim to brush them every day. They will need clipping every 6 weeks in the summer and every trip to the groomer should be followed by a fuss and a treat.

Passports aren't necessary for your dog unless you plan to travel internationally and take your dog with you. To get a passport for your dog, it needs to be vaccinated against rabies and blood tested, it needs to be micro chipped and treated for tapeworm. The rabies vaccination is £41 and the passport will cost you £15 on top of this. In the USA; you don't need a passport as such to travel abroad with your dog, but they need a health check and quarantine, which can cost upwards of $700. Passports are an avoidable expense as your dog doesn't need to travel abroad with you, and are usually more stressed by air travel than a stay in kennels.

Without the unnecessary and assuming you have your dog insured (a much cheaper option) the cost per year of keeping a Cavachon averages out at about £110 per month or $190 a month. This is on top of the other expenses like de-sexing, micro chipping and purchase price, which comes to an average of £600 for a female or £640 for a male, or $920 for a female and $1260 for a male. Although it is impossible to accurately estimate what the cost of owning every Cavachon might be because unexpected medical problems might arise that would not otherwise be considered average, and you may like to buy fancy clothes for your dog every week, when thinking about sharing your life with a dog, it's important to consider more than just the daily cost of feeding your Cavachon.

Many humans do not think about whether or not they can truly afford to care for a dog before they bring one home, and not being prepared can cause stress and problems later on.

Remember that being financially responsible for your Cavachon is a large part of being a good guardian.

Beyond the initial investment of purchasing your Cavachon puppy from a reputable breeder, for most guardians, owning a Cavachon will include the costs associated with the following:

• Food
• Treats
• Pee pads, poop bags, potty patches
• Leashes and collars
• Safety harnesses
• Travel kennels or bags
• House training pens

- Clothing
- Toys
- Beds
- Grooming
- Regular veterinary care
- Obedience or dog whispering classes
- Pet sitting, walking or boarding
- Pet insurance
- Yearly licensing
- Unexpected emergencies

As you can see, depending upon where you shop, what type of food you feed your Cavachon, what sort of veterinarian or grooming care you choose, whether or not you have pet insurance and what types of items you purchase for your Cavachon's wellbeing, the yearly cost of owning a Cavachon can vary a lot.

Other contributing factors that may have an effect on the overall yearly cost of owning a Cavachon can include the region where you live, the accessibility of the items you need, your own lifestyle and your Cavachon's age and individual needs.

5. Other animals

Other animals can do really well with Cavachons and they can do really well with other animals. If they are well socialised then these lovely, small dogs can live happily with cats, rabbits, and other dogs. Dogs are pack animals; even modern indoor pets have that real base need for company, and dogs will make their pack out of anything, including cats. Cats are good at putting little dogs like Cavachons in their place. You might have to be careful with older dogs or rescue dogs and do introductions slowly. The way you introduce Cavachons to other animals is by encouraging calm, submissive behaviour and correcting obsession or fixation, as this can lead to dangerous interest.

6. Health benefits of dogs

Humans have known for hundreds of years that it's good to have pets around. Now science is catching up and beginning to explain why. Stroking a cat or dog has a soothing effect, and dog owners have a dopamine response to their animals. The responsibility of pet ownership has generally shown a strong stabilizing effect on mood and behaviour. Studies have shown that owning a pet can increase the levels of endorphins in the brain and can increase physical health, improve sleep patterns and stave off illness. Pets can reduce the symptoms of depression. The soothing, repetitive action of stroking a pet has been proven to lower blood pressure.

7. How do Cavachons fit in with this?

Dog are wonderful for humans. In fact, we evolved with each other. Dogs likely became domesticated when curious wolves began to loiter near Stone Age people, who left butchered meat remnants littering their camps. Humans and dogs have changed each other over time. As we began to keep dogs, we relied less and less on our own senses to hunt and to defend our tribes. This allowed our brains to grow for other uses. This is called parallel evolution. The theory of parallel evolution is being studied all over the world, including at the University of Chicago.

Dogs like Cavachons also have a chemical effect on humans, just as humans have a chemical effect on dogs. Levels of oxytocin, beta-endorphin, prolactin, beta-phenylethylamine, and dopamine are massively increased by positive interactions between dogs and humans. These chemicals are all associated with happiness and calmness.

If you find yourself becoming isolated, pets, particularly ones that require you to walk them in the park a couple of times a day with other people doing the same thing, make a great ice breaker. Dog walkers will often know the names of the other dogs walking at their park. They will recognize the owners without the dogs and refer to them as "Shadow's mum" or "Max's people". Dog people are drawn to each other and dogs are a very good way to take yourself out of isolated loneliness. Pets can really push you to social interaction in ways that you are not being negatively judged. The depth of the bond between a dog and it's people means that they make great companion animals.

It's strange, but even when you struggle to take care of yourself emotionally, having a dependant who relies on you to get out of bed and feed and cuddle it "can help give you a sense of your own value and importance", according to Dr Ian Cook, director of the Depression Research (UCLA).

The uncomplicated nature of the bond between a dog and their person can be a great antidote to complex family and social relationships.

Having a routine with your Cavachon can add structure to your day and this is a fantastic way to keep your mental health on track. Dogs need a strong structure and regular walking. These are both things that are good for you. Routine and exercise are good for *your* physical and mental health.

8. Cavachons and other animals

One thing you'll know about dogs is that they are pack animals. One question a lot of people want answering when they get a dog is: do they need two? The simple answer is that you don't need any other dogs in the immediate pack – you can be enough pack for your Cavachon. Very nervous dogs can be brought out of their shell by other dogs, but you won't usually need to have more than one dog at home.

When you meet other dogs in the park you should stay calm and keep the dog calm. If your dog shows any signs of aggression you need to snap them out of it. You can do this by a quick, sharp pull upwards or to the side or by a tap on the side. This lets your dog know that aggression isn't on. If you are calm and assertive, your dog will know that you are in charge and will protect them – they will feel safe.

Dogs of this size can be a pest to cats in the household, but they can be very good with them too. As long as the dog knows that the cat is a member of the pack and is corrected for barking or being too interested in the cat then the relationship between a dog and a cat can be very positive. Most cats will put a dog in it's place with a bat on the nose – this is a normal and positive thing, a cat swatting a dog a couple of time is fine. Some cats train their dogs very well – an Alsatian/ Husky cross named Kane has a cat/ boss who will ride around on his head. Even stereotypically yappy dogs like pugs can get along fine with cats.

9. Different colours and patterns

One of the joys of the Cavachon is the wide variety of colours and patterns that are available. The Blenheim colouring and patterning is a symmetrical colouring on the ears, occasionally extending to a mask across the eyes. This colour and pattern is always apricot on white. Sable is a combination of red, tan and apricot with splashes of black. Cavachons can come in sable or sable and white. Again, this pattern is also symmetrical. Then there is the cute Tri Colour, which is black and apricot on a predominantly white background. Another colour that is very popular is Golden or Blond. This is where you have very light apricot, blond and gold fur mixed in with the white, making very pale puppies. As always, these patterns are symmetrical. The final colour combination is black and tan. This normally consists of tan coloured chops, feet and eyebrows with some also having a tan chest and tail markings on a black base. They also come in solid colours like White, Apricot, Black and Red. Because of the strict symmetry of the King Charles Cavalier, and the plain white of the Bichon Frise, Cavachons are usually pale and symmetrically marked.
Cavachons have curly to very curly fur that is long and silky. Because they don't shed very much when they are adults, they are often suggested for people with allergies, but keep in mind they will shed all of their puppy fur.

Chapter 2) Choosing your dog

It goes without saying that no dog, however trustworthy, should ever be left alone with young children. This is not a fussy thing to say, it's a safety issue and even the nicest dog can turn when it's had enough of a little one pulling its fur with his/her sticky hands. They need regular exercise but not as much as a larger dog. They should live in your house with you (they aren't suited to being yard dogs) and because of their diminutive stature and funny little faces there would be little point in trying to keep them for that purpose anyway. They are the perfect dogs for families where there is someone in a lot of the time, as they aren't as independent as some other breeds and need a lot of company. They are very good for allergy sufferers as once they are adults they don't shed very much at all. They do still shed, but regular grooming etc. can remove that as an issue.

The provenance of your dog, or where it comes from, can make all the difference to the overall experience you have with your dog. You could end up having this dog for 18 years, so it is a good idea to put a lot of time and consideration into where your dog comes from. A dog with the wrong background can be an absolute nightmare, and very stressful for you, your family and any visitors to the house, as well as to the dog. If the provenance of the dog is poor, report the conditions, don't try to 'rescue' the dog by buying it. If you start out with the right dog you can end up with a truly wonderful companion.

Firstly, where is the dog coming from? If you are buying a puppy, you want to see that it has been raised in a home environment, or had daily access to one. Farmed puppies usually tend to be badly socialized, uncomfortable around the home and stressed around people. It is important to see the mother to make sure her that welfare seems good. While her health is not your responsibility, it will affect the behavior and health of your puppy. She should be clean, free of flees or lice and have clean bedding. She should have access to fresh water and food, especially if she is still nursing. The most important thing about the mother is her behaviour. Her puppies will have learned everything they know so far from their mother and if she cowers or is uncomfortable around people, there is a strong chance the puppies will be the same, to some degree.

Farmed puppies tend to be badly socialized, uncomfortable around the home and stressed around people. If you've already got a puppy and thought it was coming from a nice home environment, but it later turns out that it was a farmed puppy, you can do something about this – it needn't be the end of the road for you and your dog, but be prepared to fix chewing and socialization problems.

Adult dogs of "unknown provenance" (trainer speak for we don't know where they came from) can be a little more tricky to judge. We know that not all beaten dogs become aggressive and that not all strays were abused, but we can't know about their trust in humans. This is where experts, like RSPCA officers or people who work at dog homes, come in really handy. They will know from spending time with the animals and by conducting a few behaviour tests how the dog should be. Most of the time, if a dog is recommended for re-homing, it will be a safe animal, although sometimes mistakes are made. My sister rescued a dog, and she and her son became very attached to her, but they were told she was very good with other dogs. The truth of the matter was she was un-walkable because of her aggression and the decision was made to send her back. They realized that they did not have the time or the expertise to give Stella what she needed in order to make her into a happy dog. There is no shame in deciding that you can't do it.

Adult dogs coming from a home where there was a good atmosphere but for whatever reason the current owners can't take care of them any more are generally a fairly safe bet. These dogs usually tend to be well socialized and at least a little trained.

RSPCA dogs can be a good idea. Maybe if you want a Cavachon as a companion and don't have masses of energy, and older dog from a rescue home that is already trained and socialized and has seen everything already so doesn't get over excited could be just what you're after. Believe it or not, there are designer cross breeds like Cavachons in dogs homes all over the place – you just have to look hard and be patient.

Now that you are happy with where the dog is coming from, you need to make sure that they are the right dog for you. Some basic sociability checks need to be done before you pick. You certainly shouldn't choose based on liking the brown and white one better than the black and white one. An unfriendly dog is unfriendly however pretty they are! Spend a little time with the dogs. Do they come straight up to you? If so, are you looking for a precocious dog? Do they hang back? Is this because they're afraid or just a little nervous? (or are they distracted by their food, which will make them easier to train?) Do you like the personality of a particular dog? This is really the most important thing. There will be one dog who just steals your heart. The feeling is probably mutual.

So you've found the right personality fit, now you need to worry about health.

Poor early nutrition and poor health can lead to poor brain development, leaving you with a dog that is difficult to train. Make sure a puppy's legs aren't bandy (bowed or curved out at the knees). This may be hard to tell if it's a little wriggler, but you need to try and see. Bandy legs can be a sign of poor early nutrition and calcium deficiency, which can cause all sorts of pain and problems. The feet should face forward - that is the claws should face forward with the pads on the ground. If this isn't the case then the tendons are not properly developed and the dog won't thrive. You should feel the body. You may be able to feel some bones through the muscle – this is normal, but you should not be able to feel the sides of any bones. The spine should not be sticking up.

Look at the eyes; is there any cloudiness or scaring? In puppies, there should be no scaring or scratches in the eyes whatsoever. This could be the sign of some health complaint other than poor eyesight that can also make a dog hard to train, or hint at long-term medical expenses.

Check the gums and ears. The gums should be pink and fleshy. White gums are a sign of anemia. Receding gums can be a sign of malnutrition or tooth problems. Ears should be clean and free from dirt or flee droppings. There should be no discharge from the ears.

If you see a puppy in a pet shop that seems miserable, don't buy it. You are not rescuing it; you are enabling bad practice from the pet shop. DO NOT BUY A PUPPY TO RESCUE IT FROM A PET SHOP. Report the shop; don't saddle yourself with an unhealthy, unhappy animal. This can cause a lot of heartache for both you and the dog. There are lots of very good, reputable pet shops, but animals from bad pet shops can have a whole host of health, emotional and behavioral problems that you can do without. If you are worried about the health of a dog or puppy, inform the authorities. They will have people with the knowledge and experience to deal with any physical and psychological problems.

As soon as a new hybrid, mixed breed or *"designer dog"* becomes popular, they also become particularly susceptible to being bred by disreputable, high profit puppy farms or "commercial breeders".

The puppy farm is a brutal and cruel world of canine pregnancy for profit and occurs all over the world, and if you aren't very careful about where and how you purchase your Cavachon puppy, you may unknowingly end up promoting this disreputable practice.

Not only do puppy farms seriously contribute to overpopulation, they produce diseases and genetically flawed puppies that may suffer greatly with behavioral and/or health related problems that will cost their guardians greatly in terms grief and stress and the unexpected financial burden associated with veterinarian and behavioural costs, while the puppy's life may be cut prematurely short.

These dogs suffer in ways most of us could never imagine. For instance, most of these poor bred dogs have never walked on solid ground or felt grass as they are housed in cramped, wire cages their entire short lives.

Females are bred continuously until they can no longer produce puppies, at which time they are sold to laboratories for experiments, killed or dumped on the side of a road. This is no way to live. Their health is usually poor and their bodies are exhausted. They are un-socialized, their mental health needs aren't met and they become afraid of humans and generally neurotic.

Although the puppy farm problem is certainly not exclusive to the United States, as it happens all over the world, the problem is so rampant in the United States that several states are actually labeled as puppy mill states. These include Missouri, Nebraska, Kansas, Iowa, Arkansas, Oklahoma and Pennsylvania.

It can be difficult to shut down these mill operations because, just like the drug trade, it is business on a large and lucrative scale. As an example, in Missouri alone, it is estimated that the commercial puppy breeding industry nets $40 million dollars (£24,068,800) a year.

Although puppy farm puppies are sold in a variety of different venues, pet stores are the main source for selling these unfortunate puppies, who are taken away from their mothers far too young (at 4 to 5 weeks of age) and sold to brokers, who pack them into crates to ship them off to pet stores. Many innocent puppies die during transportation.

Think seriously before buying a puppy from a pet store because almost all puppies found in pet stores are the result of inhumane puppy farm breeding, and if you purchase one of these puppies, you are helping to enable and perpetuate this horribly cruel breeding practice.

Every time someone buys a puppy from a pet store, the store will order more from the puppy farm. As far as the pet store is concerned, the puppies are simply inventory, like bags of dog food, and when one item drops off of the inventory list, another is purchased to replace it.

Puppy mill puppies are also sold at flea markets, on the side of the road, at the beach, through newspaper ads and through fancy websites and Internet classifieds.

The only way to put these shameful, commercial businesses out of business is by spreading the word and never buying a puppy from a pet store, or any other advertising medium, unless you have first thoroughly checked them out by visiting the facility in person.

Always be wary if you answer an advertisement for a puppy for sale and the person selling offers to deliver the puppy to you, because this could easily be the first sign that you are about to be involved in an illegal puppy mill operation.

Educate yourself and spread the word to others about puppy mills, because this is the first step towards ensuring that yourself and everyone you know are never unknowingly involved in the suffering that is forced upon the breeding dogs and puppies trapped in a puppy mill operation.

1. Questions to ask a breeder

Get to know your breeder by asking them why they decided to breed Cavachons and how long they have been breeding for.

Ask if the breeder will permit you to visit their facility and will they give you a tour?

Ask if the breeder is familiar with or worked closely with both parents of the Cavachon puppy?

Ask how often the breeder allows the females and males to breed and reproduce?

Ask if the breeder allows you to see the other dogs in the kennel and notice whether the kennel is clean, well-maintained and animal friendly.

Will the breeder permit you to see other adult dogs, or other puppies that the breeder owns, socialize together?

Pay attention to whether the breeder limits the amount of time that you are permitted to handle the Cavachon puppies. A reputable breeder will be concerned for the safety and health of all their puppies and will only permit serious buyers to handle the puppies.

Check to find out if the breeder is recognized by your local, state or national breed organization.

a) Medical Questions

Every reputable breeder will certainly ensure that their Cavachon puppies have received vaccinations and de-worming specific to the age of the puppies. Always ask the breeder what shots the puppy has received and when it was last de-wormed. Ask for the name of the breeder's veterinarian.

If you discover that the breeder has not carried out any of these procedures or they are unable to tell you when the last shots or de-worming was carried out, look elsewhere.

Also ask to see the breeder's veterinarian report on the health of the puppy you may be interested in purchasing, and if they cannot produce this report, look elsewhere.

b) Temperament Questions

You will want to choose a puppy with a friendly, easy going and congenial temperament and your breeder should be able to help you with your selection.

A good breeder will have noticed personality and temperament traits very early on in their Cavachon puppies and should be able to provide a prospective purchaser with valuable insight concerning each puppy's unique personality.

Also ask the breeder about the temperament and personalities of the puppy's parents and if they have socialized the puppies.

Always be certain to ask if a Cavachon puppy you are interested in has displayed any signs of aggression or fear, because if this is happening at such an early age, you may experience behavioral troubles when the puppy becomes older.

c) Guarantee Questions

A reputable Cavachon breeder will be interested in the lifelong health and wellbeing of all of their puppies and good breeders will want you to call them should a problem arise at any time during the life of your Cavachon puppy.

As well, a good breeder will want you to return a puppy or dog to them, if for some reason you are unable to continue to care for it, rather than seeing the dog go to a shelter or rescue facility.

If the Cavachon breeder you are considering does not offer this type of return policy, find one who does, because no ethical breeder would ever permit one of his or her puppies to end up in a shelter.

d) Return Contract

Reputable breeders offer return contracts. They do this to protect their reputation and to also make sure that a puppy they have sold that might display a genetic defect will not have the opportunity to breed and continue to spread the defect, which could weaken the entire breed.

Breeders also offer return contracts because purchasing a hybrid Cavachon puppy from a breeder can be an expensive proposition, and if you find out that the puppy has a worrisome genetic defect, this could cost you a great deal with respect to unexpected veterinarian care. In such cases, most good breeders offer a returns policy, and will be happy to give you another puppy.

e) Testimonials

Ask a Cavachon breeder you are considering to provide you with testimonials from some of their previous clients, and then actually contact those people to ask them about their experience with the breeder, and the health and temperament of their Cavachon dog.

A good breeder has nothing to hide and will be more than happy to provide you with testimonials because their best recommendation is a happy customer.

f) Breeder Reputation

The Internet can be a valuable resource when researching the reputation of a Cavachon breeder. For instance, you will be able to post on most forums discussing breeders to quickly find out what you need to know from those who have first hand experience.

In addition, be prepared to answer questions the breeder may have for you, because a reputable breeder will want to ask a prospective purchaser their own questions, so that they can satisfy themselves that you are going to be a good caretaker for their puppy.

Firstly, do your homework about the Cavachon breed and then carry out as much research as possible about the specific breeder before making your initial visit to their facility.

The more information you have gathered about the Cavachon hybrid, as well as the breeder, and the more information the breeder knows about you, the more successful the match will be.

2. Where to purchase a puppy

USA

When wondering where to start your search for purchasing a Cavachon puppy in the United States, there are several clubs and registries that will be good starting points, including:

- **American Canine Hybrid Club** (ACHC) is a hybrid registry service established in 1969.

- **National Hybrid Registry** (NHR) The NHR is a registry service for dog's from which both parents are verified to be pure-bred dogs and eligible to be registered in the National Kennel Club.

- **International Designer Canine Registry®** (IDCR) is the World's Premier Designer Dog Registry and is dedicated exclusively to providing certified registration and pedigree services for all designer breeds. The IDCR also provides a list of registered breeders.

UK

Little Rascals *"takes great pride in being able to breed a varied range of pedigree and designer crossbreed puppies for sale to customers throughout Lincoln and the UK. As specialized licensed dog breeders we have almost 50 years experience in breeding, so you can be certain that a puppy from us has been given the best possible care and start in life."*
www.littlerascalsuk.com

Designer Dogs - The Kennel Club is a registration and information service to help prospective owners find Kennel Club "assured breeders".
www.thekennelclub.org.uk

You will find more breeders and breeders in Australia in the Resources section of this book.

www.petfinder.com is another useful resource.

Chapter 3) Puppies

When they are very young and as they get a bit doddery and old, Cavachons, like people, require different, specific care.

1. Check if your puppy is healthy

Of course you will want to check if a puppy you are considering taking home is not just emotionally healthy, but also physically healthy.

Firstly, ask to see veterinarian reports from the breeder to satisfy yourself that the puppy is as healthy as possible, and then once you make your decision to share your life with a particular puppy, make an appointment with your own veterinarian for a complete examination.

Before you get to this stage, however, there are a few general signs of good health to be aware of when choosing a healthy puppy from a litter, including the following:

- **Breathing**: they will breathe quietly, without coughing or sneezing, and there will be no crusting or discharge around their nostrils;

- **Body**: they will look round and well-fed, with an obvious layer of fat over their rib cage;

- **Coat**: they will have a soft, shiny coat with no dandruff, dullness, greasiness or bald spots;

- **Energy**: a well-rested puppy should be alert and energetic;

- **Hearing**: a puppy should react if you clap your hands behind their head;

- **Genitals**: they will not have any sort of discharge visible in or around their genital or anal region;

- **Mobility**: they will walk and run normally without wobbling, limping or seeming to be stiff or sore;

- **Vision**: they will have bright, clear eyes without crust or discharge and they should notice a ball rolling past within their field of vision.

2. One Cavachon or Two?

While getting two Cavachon puppies at once will be double the fun, it will also be double the work, which means as their human guardian (you) will need to be doubly alert and patient, and perhaps also lose even more sleep than you bargained for during the potty training phase.

Every puppy needs your constant attention and guidance, therefore, before taking the plunge, ask yourself if you have the time and energy to provide constant attention and guidance for two little puppies?

Many humans decide to get two puppies because they want their puppy to have someone to play with, and one of the reasons for this decision might be based on the fact that the human making this decision might not be the ideal candidate for having one puppy, let alone two.

For instance, if the reason you are considering two puppies is so that the one puppy will not be alone all day while you are at work, stop right there, because leaving one, two or a dozen puppies alone all day while you are at work is a terrible decision and you should NOT be considering any puppy at this stage of your life.

Another consideration when thinking about whether or not to get two puppies is that often when they grow up, there may be continual sibling rivalry as each puppy vies for your attention.

What often happens when the puppies mature is that they stop getting along with each other, and their relationship may deteriorate to the point where they no longer enjoy each other's company.

Furthermore, when you have two puppies growing up together, one will always be the more dominant personality that will take over the other, and this could mean that neither puppy will fully develop their individual personalities.

In addition, when you have two puppies or dogs in your life, they generally tend to be less affectionate or interested in their human guardians as they have each other in their own pack of dogs to rely upon. This can mean that they will focus so much on each other that they will bond much less with you, which can make it more difficult to train or convince either that you are the actual leader of the pack.

Each puppy will require your individual attention when it comes time for training, and having two puppies in the picture can make it very difficult for them to concentrate or focus on the job at hand.

For instance, when you are teaching puppy #1 to "Sit" and puppy #2 is trying to bite their tail, your job is going to be much more challenging. The only way to properly accomplish training sessions with two puppies will be to lock one of the puppies in another room so that they each have their one on one time with you.

Bottom line is, most professional trainers will advise that if you want two puppies, don't to get them at the exact same time or from the same litter, so that you have the opportunity to house train and teach basic commands to one puppy before you bring another one into the home.

3. Puppy Proofing Your Home

Most puppies will be a curious bundle of energy, which means that they will get into everything within their reach.

As a responsible puppy guardian, you will want to provide a safe environment for them, which means eliminating all sources of danger, similar to what you would do for a curious toddler.

Be aware that your Cavachon puppy will want to touch, sniff, taste, investigate and closely inspect every electrical cord, every closet, every nook and cranny of your home and everything you may have left lying about on the floor.

Power cords can be found in just about every room in the home and to a teething puppy, these may look like irresistible, fun chew toys. Make sure that you tuck all power cords securely out of your puppy's reach or enclose them inside a chew-proof PVC tube.

Kitchen: first of all, there are many human foods that can be harmful to dogs, therefore, your kitchen should always be strictly off limits to your puppy any time you are preparing food. Calmly send them out of the kitchen any time you are in the kitchen, and they will quickly get the idea that this area is off limits to them.

Bathroom: bathroom cupboards and drawers or the side of a bathtub where you may leave your shaving supplies can hold many dangers for a young and curious Cavachon puppy.

Kleenex, cotton swabs, Q-tips, toilet paper, razors, pills, and soap left within your puppy's reach are an easy target that could result in an emergency visit to your veterinarian's office.

Family members need to put shampoos, soap, facial products, makeup and accessories out of reach or safely inside a cabinet or drawer.

Bedroom: if you don't keep your shoes, slippers and clothing safely behind closed doors, you may find that your puppy has claimed them for their new chew toys. Be vigilant about keeping everything in its safe place, including jewellery, hair ties, bills, coins, and other items small enough for them to swallow in containers or drawers, and secure any exposed cords or wires.

If you have children, make sure they understand that, especially while your puppy is going through their teething stage, they must keep their rooms picked up and leave nothing that could cause a choking problem to the puppy lying about on the floor or within their reach.

Living Room: we humans often spend many hours in our cosy gathering places to watch movies or play games, and often the living areas of our homes will have many items that are very enticing for a curious and teething puppy, such as books, magazines, pillows, iPods, TV remotes and more.

You will want to keep your home free of excess clutter and remain vigilant about straightening up and putting things out of sight that could be tempting to your puppy.

Office: we humans often spend a great deal of time in our home offices, which means that our puppy will want to be there too, and they will be curious about all the items an office has to offer, including papers, books, magazines, and electrical cords.

Although your puppy might think that rubber bands or paper clips are fun to play with, allowing these items to be within your puppy's reach could end up being a fatal mistake if your puppy swallows them.

Plants: these are also a very tempting target for your puppy's teeth, so you will want to keep them well out of their reach. If you have floor plants, they will need to be moved to a shelf or counter or placed behind a closed door until your curious fur friend grows out of the habit of putting everything in their mouth. Also keep in mind that many common houseplants are poisonous to dogs.

Garage and Yard: there are obvious as well as subtle dangers that could seriously harm or even kill a Cavachon puppy that are often found in the garage or yard. Some of these might include antifreeze, gasoline, fertilizers, rat and mice poison, snail and slug poison, weed killer, paint, cleaners and solvents, grass seed, bark mulch and various insecticides.

If you are storing any of these toxic substances in your garage or garden shed, make certain that you keep all such bottles, boxes, or containers inside a locked cabinet, or stored on high shelves that your puppy will not be able to reach. Even better, choose not to use toxic chemicals anywhere in your home or yard.

Puppy Hazard Home Inspection

Every conscientious puppy guardian needs to take a serious look around the home, not just from the human eye level, but from the eye level of a Cavachon puppy. This means literally crawling around your floors.

Your puppy has a much lower vantage point than you do when standing, therefore, there may be items in your environment that could potentially be harmful to a Cavachon puppy that a human might not notice unless you get down on the floor and take a really good look.

4. First Weeks With Your Puppy

a) The First Night

Before you go to the breeder's to pick up your new Cavachon puppy, vacuum your floors and do a last minute check of every room to make sure that everything that could be a puppy hazard is carefully tucked away out of sight and that nothing is left on the floor or low down on shelves where a curious puppy might get into trouble.

Close most of the doors inside your home, so that there are just one or two rooms that the puppy will have access to.

You have already been shopping and have everything you need, so get out a puppy pee pad and have it at the ready when you bring your new furry friend home.

Also have your soft bed(s) in an area where you will be spending most of your time and where they will be easily found by your puppy. If you have already purchased a soft toy, leave it in your puppy's soft bed, or take the toy with you when you go to pick up your puppy.

NOTE: take either your hard-sided kennel or your soft-sided "Sherpa" travel bag with you when going to bring your new Cavachon puppy home, and make sure that it is securely fastened to the seat of your vehicle with the seatbelt system and lined with a puppy pee pad.

Even though you will be tempted to hold your new Cavachon puppy in your lap on the drive home, this is a very dangerous place for them to be, in case of an accident.

Place them inside their kennel or bag, which will be lined with soft towels and perhaps even a warm, towel-wrapped hot water bottle, and close the door. If you have a friend who can drive for you, sit beside them in the back seat, and if they cry on the way home, remind them that they are not alone with your soft, soothing voice.

Before bringing your new Cavachon puppy inside your home, take them to the place where you want them to relieve themselves and try to wait it out long enough for them to at least go pee.

Then bring them inside your home and introduce them to the area where their food and water bowls will be kept, in case they are hungry or thirsty.

Let them wander around, sniffing and checking out their new surroundings and gently encourage them to follow you wherever you go.

Show them where the puppy pee pad is located and place it near the door where you will exit to take them outside to relieve themselves. Many pee pads are scented to encourage a puppy to pee, and if they do, happily praise them.

Show them where their hard-sided kennel is (in your bedroom) and put them inside with the door open while you sit on the floor in front and quietly encourage them to relax inside their kennel.

Depending on the time of day when you bring your new Cavachon puppy home for the first time, practice this kennel exercise several times throughout the day, and if they will take a little treat each time you encourage them to go inside their kennel, this will help to further encourage the behaviour of wanting to go inside.

After they have had their evening meal, take them outside approximately 20 minutes later to relieve themselves, and when they do, make sure you are very enthusiastic with your praise and perhaps even give a little treat.

So far your Cavachon puppy has only been allowed in several rooms of your home, as you have kept the other doors closed, so keep it this way for the first few days.

Before it's time for bed, again take your puppy outside for a very short walk to the same place where they last relieved themselves and make sure that they go pee before bringing them back inside.

Before bed, prepare your Cavachon puppy's hot water bottle and wrap it in a towel so that it will not be too hot for them, and place it inside their hard-sided kennel (in your bedroom).

Turn the lights down low and invite your puppy to go inside their kennel and if they seem interested, perhaps give them a soft toy to have inside with them. Let them walk into the kennel under their own steam and when they do, give them a little treat (if they are interested) and encourage them to snuggle down to sleep while you are sitting on the floor in front of the kennel.

Once they have settled down inside their kennel, close the door, go to your bed and turn all the lights off. It may help your puppy to sleep during their first night home, if you can play quiet, soothing music in the background.

If they start to cry or whine, stay calm and have compassion because this is the first time in their young life when they do not have the comfort of their mother or their litter mates. Do not let them out of their kennel, simply reassure them with your calm voice that they are not alone until they fall asleep.

b) The First Week

During the first week, you and your new Cavachon puppy will be getting settled into their new routine, which will involve you getting used to your puppy's needs as they also get used to your usual schedule.

Be as consistent as possible with your waking and sleeping routine, getting up and going to bed at the same time each day, so that it will be easier for your puppy to get into the flow of their new life.

First thing in the morning, remove your puppy from their kennel and take them immediately outside to relieve themselves at the place where they last went pee.

At this time, if you are teaching them to ring a doorbell to go outside, let them ring the bell before you go out the door with them, whether you are carrying them, or whether they are walking out the door on their own.

NOTE: during the first week, you may want to carry your puppy outside first thing in the morning as they may not be able to hold it for very long once waking up.

When you bring them back inside, you can let them follow you so they get used to their new leash and/or harness arrangement.

Be very careful not to drag your puppy if they stop or pull back on the leash. If they refuse to walk on the leash, just hold the tension toward you (without pulling) while encouraging them to walk towards you, until they start to move forward again.

Now it will be time for their first feed of the day, and after they have finished eating, keep an eye on the clock, because you will want to take them outside to relieve themselves in about 20 minutes.

When your puppy is not eating or napping, they will be wanting to explore and have little play sessions with you and these times will help you bond with your puppy more and more each day.

As their new guardian, it will be your responsibility to keep a close eye on them throughout the day, so that you can notice when they need to relieve themselves and either take them to their pee pad or take them outside.

You will also need to make sure that they are eating and drinking enough throughout the day, so set regular feeding times at least three times a day.

Also set specific times in the day when you will take your puppy out for a little walk on a leash and harness, so that they are not only going outside when they need to relieve themselves, but they are also learning to explore their new neighbourhood with you beside them.

When your Cavachon puppy is still very young, you will not want to walk for a long time as they will get tired easily, so keep your walks to no more than 15 or 20 minutes during your first week and if they seem tired or cold, pick them up and carry them home.

5. Common Mistakes to Avoid

a) Sleeping in Your Bed

Many of us humans make the mistake of allowing a crying puppy to sleep with us in bed, and while this may help to calm and comfort a new puppy, it will set a dangerous precedent that can result in behavioural problems later on in their life.

As well, a sleeping human body can easily crush a tiny Cavachon puppy.

As much as it may pull on your heart strings to hear your new Cavachon puppy crying the first couple of nights in their kennel, a little tough love at the beginning will help them to learn to both love and respect you as their leader.

b) Picking Them Up at the Wrong Time

Never pick your puppy up if they display fear or growl at an object or person, because this will be rewarding them for unbalanced behaviour.

Instead, your puppy needs to be gently corrected by you, with firm and calm energy so that they learn not to react with fear or aggression.

c) Playing Too Hard or Too Long

Many humans play too hard or allow their children to play too long with a young puppy. You need to remember that a young puppy tires very easily and especially during the critical growing phases of their young life, they need their rest.

d) Hand Play

Always discourage your Cavachon puppy from chewing or biting your hands, or any part of your body for that matter. If you allow them to do this when they are puppies, they will want to continue to do so when they have strong jaws and adult teeth and this is not acceptable behaviour for any breed of dog.

Do not get into the habit of playing the *"hand"* game, where you rough up the puppy and slide them across the floor with your hands, because this will teach your puppy that your hands are playthings.

When your puppy is teething, they will naturally want to chew on everything within reach, and this will include you. As cute as you might think it is, this is not an acceptable behaviour and you need to gently, but firmly, discourage the habit.

A light flick with a finger on the end of a puppy nose, combined with a firm "NO" when they are trying to bite human fingers will discourage them from this activity.

e) Distraction and Replacement

When your puppy tries to chew on your hand, foot, clothing or anything else that is not fair game, you need to firmly and calmly tell them "No", and then distract them by replacing what they are not supposed to be chewing with their chew toy.

Make sure that you happily praise them every time they choose the toy to chew on.

If the puppy persists in chewing on you, remove yourself from the equation by getting up and walking away. If they are really persistent, put them inside their kennel with a favourite chew toy until they calm down.

Always praise your puppy when they stop inappropriate behaviour so that they begin to understand what they can and cannot do.

6. Bonding With Your Cavachon

You will begin bonding with your Cavachon puppy from the very first moment you bring them home from the breeders.

This is the time when your puppy will be the most distraught as they will no longer have the guidance, warmth and comfort of their mother or their other litter mates, and you will need to take on the role of being your new puppy's centre of attention.

Be patient and kind with them as they are learning that you are now their new centre of the universe.

Your daily interaction with your puppy during play sessions and especially your disciplined exercises, including going for walks on the leash, and teaching commands and tricks, will be the best bonding opportunities.

Do not make the mistake of thinking that *"bonding"* with your new puppy can only happen if you are playing or cuddling together, because the very best bonding happens when you are kindly teaching rules and boundaries

Chapter 4) Caring for your Cavachon

You are legally responsible for your dog's welfare. There are a few things they need in everyday life. They need somewhere safe and warm to live. They need the right nutrition to keep them happy and well. They need to play games and have toys – their emotional wellbeing is your responsibility too, no one is making you get a dog.

1. Shopping list

Before bringing home your new Cavachon for the first time, there will be a list of items you need to make sure you have on hand, including:

- **Food** - usually the puppy will remain on whatever food they have been fed at the breeder's for at least the first couple of weeks, until they are well settled in their new home, so make sure you ask the breeder what brand to buy;

- **Food and Water Bowls** - make sure they are small enough for a young Cavachon puppy to get into so that they can easily eat and drink. Suggest a durable stainless dining set that can later be used as travel bowls;

- **Kennel** - when you buy your puppy's hard-sided kennel, make sure that you buy the size that will be appropriate for them when they are fully grown. It must be large enough so that (when fully grown) they can easily stand up and turn around inside it;

- **Martingale collar, 2 Leashes and Harness** - buy the harness and collar small enough to fit your puppy and buy new ones as they grow larger. You will be able to keep the same leashes as all you will ever need is a four foot (1.22 meters) leash made out of nylon webbing, with a lightweight clip at the end (do not buy a leash that has a heavy clip on the end as it will be difficult for your tiny puppy to carry around);

- **Soft beds** (one or two) for them to sleep in when they are not in their kennel - get the beds large enough for a full grown Cavachon;

- *"Sherpa"* or another type of soft-sided travel bag to get them used to travelling inside a carrier bag - get the bag large enough to fit them when they are fully grown and take it with you when you pick up your puppy from the breeder;

- **Shampoo and Conditioner;**

- **Finger tooth brush** - this is a soft, rubber cap that fits over the human's finger to get the puppy used to having their teeth regularly brushed;

- **Soft bristle brush and comb** - for daily grooming;

- **Puppy nail scissors** - for trimming their toenails;

- **Small, blunt nosed grooming scissors** - for trimming the hair around their eyes;

- **One or two soft toys**, or wait until they come home and let them pick their own toys from the store;

- **Puppy sized treats;**

- **Poop bags;**

- **Pee pads;**

- **Bath towels;**

- **Non-slip mat for the sink or tub.**

Be sure to take your Cavachon shopping list with you when you go to your local pet store or boutique, otherwise you may forget critical items.

2. Housing requirements

Cavachons need to be indoor dogs; they can't live in the yard in a kennel, as they are too small and vulnerable to the elements. Your dog needs it's own bed, they need to know that their bed is their bed and that it won't be disturbed and that they are safe there. Dogs in your home need to be able to get cool on hot days and warm on cool days, so a soft dog bed on a tilled or laminate floor is the perfect place – they can lie on the floor to cool themselves and in their bed to get warm. They need to know where they are and aren't allowed to be – sofa's, bedrooms etc. They can't be left for long periods of time on their own – lonely or bored dogs can become destructive.

If you choose to crate your dog you need a crate at least big enough for them to turn around and stand up fully. A Cavachon is quite a small dog so would be happy in a medium crate. Cates should always be associated with positive things and never used as a punishment or to keep them out of the way.

Your little dog will need a bed. It needs to be their own safe place and there are a number of options, because they aren't very big.

Igloo bed

If you have a nervous dog but don't want to crate, an igloo type bed, or a fabric pyramid bed is a good idea. These are usually made for cats, but the little Cavachon will snuggle in quite happily. The little cave can make them feel so safe and confident. These are also good for very young or very old dogs as they help to keep their temperature constant.

Pads

There are lots of simple pad beds out there; these allow puppy lots of movement and freedom. If your little dog likes to stretch out on your settee with no cushions touching them or enclosing chair backs, then a pad bed will be a good start. These are generally easy to move and easy to clean.

Doughnut beds

The doughnut bed is a variation on the pad bed, but with a stuffed fabric ring around the edge to add a little bit of security. These beds are good for cats that like to stretch out in corners of the couch. Like the pad bed, they are usually easy to clean and move around.

Basket

The traditional basket is a very good, classic choice. They look good in your home and, more importantly, they are very flexible – you can move them about and take them with you when you visit friends with your dog. They have good sides to curl up against for dogs that need to feel secure. Baskets are lightweight and portable, so can go with you and your Cavachon when you go visiting.

In the end, though, your puppy will let you know where they're most comfortable sleeping.

3. Games

Fetch is a great game to play with your dog. Most dogs will learn to fetch without much effort. You have to make sure you're playing fetch with something safe and suitable to play with. Small stones and brittle sticks can be swallowed and choked on.

Agility training is great for adventurous little dogs like Cavachons. There are clubs and classes and teams you can join too, so it can help to socialize nervous dogs while they have something else to do. A job can really help with all sorts of things and agility is a good job. It also helps to bond with your dog, as well as keeping them fit and healthy.

By hiding things about the house or in the garden that smell interesting you can teach your dog to seek. The nose is the most powerful sense for all dogs, and the opportunity to use it is very good for them. They like smells like vanilla, banana and sheep poo.

You can make jumps by stacking breezeblocks or bricks on top of one another and placing strips of plywood on top. Cavachons are only little, so adjust the height of the jumps appropriately.

Tunnels are fantastic and pop-up cat tunnels are great for Cavachons, although you might need someone else to help with this one. One person holds the dog while the other person should stand at the other end and say their name followed by the command "tunnel", then the dog should be released and rewarded if they do it right. Eventually, you will be able to say the command and they will run down the tunnel.

4. Toys

Tennis Ball Launchers are great if you don't have much of an arm. They are fairly simple and relatively cheap and they can fling tennis balls quite far.

Tennis ball cannon

While an automatic ball thrower is expensive, if you are out of the house a lot then it can be a real investment. You can set it up to throw the ball 5-10 metres, at intervals of 7-15 seconds in a secure room and aim it so the ball won't hit any windows. This is a great way to keep your dog happy and stop them getting bored, frustrated and destructive. Games for when you're out, like this one, can help with dogs that feel anxious when you leave the house too.

Tug toys are a good way to test tooth health and small dogs like Cavachons like to tug at things. You should be careful not to overexcite dogs when playing tug of war, though, as it can be misinterpreted as a biting game.

Squeaky toys may be very irritating, but they are a great way for little dogs to keep themselves entertained. If they are too much for you, you can choose to only give them while you are out.

Rubber ring/flyer type things are a great toy to play fetch with as they are also good to chew, which encourages strong and healthy teeth.

Tennis balls are good fun. You can buy them very cheaply second hand and dogs will play with them on their own, bouncing them about, knocking them off walls and catching them.

Tunnels are fantastic for little dogs to run about in. Not only for agility training and games, but for dogs to play with unsupervised. They will pull their things through there and run about from one end to the other. If you have 2 dogs, they will play peek-a-boo with each other in and around the tunnel.

Interactive treat toys

Hagen dogit mind games for dogs are a strange set of devises that allow dogs to show their natural behaviours. They encourage chasing and worrying and physical exercise while at the same time making them think about where the treats are and how to get at them. You can play the game with the dog, or you can use it as a treat dispenser while you're out at work.

The Nina Ottosson Dog Tornado Interactive Game is a real stunner of a toy. It makes the dog push the sides about, using its nose to get out their prize. This is a great way to feed dogs that eat too fast too. You can use the dog tornado interactive game to help feed your dog and keep them entertained while you are out buy filling the base with dry food.

The Trixie Gamble Box Strategy Game is very entertaining for inquisitive and intelligent dogs like the Cavachon– there are very funny videos on youtube! With a combination of draws to pull and lids to lift, this is a good game for your clever little Cavachon.

The Turn Around Dog Puppy Activity Game, while for puppies, can be used by Cavachons well into adulthood. They are great for dogs who don't like to be left alone and are a good way to distract and treat your dog while you're out or about to go out.

The Snack Roll Dog Activity Game is a food or treat dispenser game. You put treats and dry food into it and the dog has to nose it about to get the food out. It is a fantastic tool for dogs that eat too fast or to feed dry food and keep them entertained while you are out.

The Kicker Dog Puzzle Treat Dispenser by trixie is another feeding toy, and has a fabulous way to get your dog to use their brain. The dog has to push leavers and move things to make the treats come out. They have to really work for it.

Treat balls of all descriptions are good for slow feeding, getting out natural worrying behaviours and for making your dog use its brain. They are simple little balls with holes in for the treats to fall out as the dog worries the ball around on the floor.

Kyjen make a Kibble Drop Game, which works in the same way as a treat ball, but is a little more challenging and so is a good alternative for dogs who get too good at treat balls.

The Activity Strategy Game Gambling Tower is another game by Trixe that is fantastic. This game requires a lot of mental energy and brainpower to get at the treats. There are three pull out shelves that the dog has to manipulate to get the treats to fall down to the bottom. There are also things to hide the treat under.

Another Trixie toy that's good at encouraging the natural digging/foraging behaviour of small dogs like Cavachons is the Mini Solitaire Dog Puzzle Treat Dispenser. It has a number of hiding cups to hide treats under. You can hide treats under all or only some of the cups. The dog can then use its nose to find the treats. This is very good for the psychological health of your dog.

5. Holiday

While you're not home your dog still needs entertaining. There are toys that your dog can play with while you're at work, but while you are on holiday they need a little more. A lot of dog owners take their dogs to kennels while they are away, but they are not necessarily ideal for every dog. Some dogs - for example very old, the very timid or those who have spent time in a Re-homing Centre - might find it a particularly stressful experience. It is important to consider if your dog would be happier in a home environment with family, friends or a pet sitter.

If you get your dog used to the idea of kennels, and that you are coming home, then your dog can do really well in kennels. Make sure you find a good boarding kennel for the first kennel your dog stays in. You need to make positive association with staying away from home. Ask people you know, local dog owners and vets about a good boarding kennel. You can also ask on forums. Preparation is the key. If you know that your dog will be well looked after you will be calm, which is best for your dog. It also avoids any negative connections with kennels.

The boarding kennels should be clean, dry and spacious. They should offer a walking service as part of the boarding costs – this shows that they know walking a dog is not optional. They should ask for vaccination proof, if they don't then the other dogs there might not be vaccinated. The other dogs there should be clean and happy. You need to make sure that their insurance will cover any emergency veterinary treatments.

If you are able to get a friend, neighbour or family member who is willing to pop in to look after your dog while you are away you should really consider giving them wine and chocolate and showering them with gifts. This way your dog will have the least upset and disturbance and their routine and entertainment can be kept up. Ask your dog sitter to walk them and feed them at the same times you do. It would be good if they could stay over at your house, but this isn't always practical. If they could stay and watch TV for an hour, or eat a meal at your house, though, this has a calming influence over the dogs, as it lets them know that everything is normal and that they are safe.

I personally wouldn't take the risk of flying with a dog. The cold in the hold isn't good for them and if you are holidaying abroad you have no way of knowing how friendly the local dogs are.

One thing that's brilliant for dogs, though, is camping trips. While some campsites don't allow dogs, most do. It is important to keep the rules in place while you're camping with a dog, but at the same time, the dog will be excited and you should embrace the closeness this gives your pack – man and beast.

In the UK, folk festivals are like a dog convention, they all get on so well and the dogs really love being with other dogs and with their extended human pack.

Chapter 5) Grooming

Grooming is a vital part of the breed specific care needed by your Cavachon. They have long, fine fur that needs daily management. Lots of Cavachon owners find that, because of the mixture of straight and curly hair, a strong comb with wide teeth is best. Brushing and combing your dog's coat is an often-overlooked task that is a necessary part of maintaining your dog's health. As well, taking time to brush and comb your Cavachon's coat will also give you an opportunity to bond with your dog, while identifying any problems (such as lumps or bumps and matted hair) early on, before they may become more serious.

Make sure that your grooming sessions are as pleasant as possible by choosing the right tools for a Cavachon and their type and length of coat. You will need a variety of brushes and combs to keep your Cavachon's coat in good condition, that will include a soft bristle brush, a slicker brush and a pin brush.

As well as your collection of brushes, you will need to invest in a metal comb, a flea comb and perhaps a mat splitter. If you always give a treat after the grooming as soon as they are calm they will learn that grooming is a positive experience. If you need to bathe your dog, make sure that you only use a tiny amount of dog shampoo – do not use human shampoo, as it is often far too harsh. The water needs to be about the same temperature as the dog, a little warmer. You need to get the dog completely dry with his or her own towel afterwards.

It will be very important to get your Cavachon puppy used to the routine of grooming early on, so that they will not be traumatized for the rest of their life, every time grooming is necessary.

Not taking the time to regularly involve your Cavachon puppy in grooming sessions could lead to serious, unwanted behaviour that may include trauma to your dog, not to mention stress or injury to you in the form of biting and scratching, that could result in a lifetime of unhappy grooming sessions.

When you neglect a regular, daily or at least weekly at home grooming session with your puppy or dog to remove tangles and keep mats to a minimum, this will not only cost you and your canine companion in terms of possible trauma and extended time on the grooming table, it will cost you a higher fee should you opt to have regular clipping and grooming carried out at a professional salon.

An effective home regimen will include not just surface brushing, but also getting to all those sensitive areas easily missed around the ears and collar area, the armpit area, and the back end and tail.

Do not allow yourself to get caught in the *"my dog doesn't like it"* trap which is an excuse many owners will use to avoid regular grooming sessions.

When you allow your dog to dictate whether they will permit a grooming session or not, you are setting a dangerous precedent that could lead to lifetime of trauma for both you and your Cavachon.

When humans neglect daily grooming routines, many dogs develop a heightened sensitivity, especially with regard to having their legs and feet held, touched, brushed or clipped and will do anything they can to avoid the process when you need to groom them.

Make a pact with yourself right from the first day you bring your puppy home never to neglect a regular grooming routine and not to avoid sensitive areas, such as trimming toenails, just because your dog may not particular *"like"* it.

1. Bath Time

Step One: before you get your Cavachon anywhere near the water, it's important to make sure that you brush out any debris, knots or tangles from their coat before you begin the bathing process because getting knots or tangles wet could make them tighter and much more difficult to remove, which will cause your dog pain and distress.

As well, removing any debris from your dog's coat beforehand, including dead undercoat and shedding hair will make the entire process easier on you, your dog, and your drains, which will become clogged with hair if you don't remove it beforehand.

Step Two: if your Cavachon has a long coat, the process will be much easier if you first spray the coat with a light mist of leave-in conditioner before brushing. This will also help to protect the delicate hair strands from breaking.

Step Three: whether you're bathing your Cavachon in your kitchen sink or your bathtub, you will always want to first lay down a rubber bath mat to provide a more secure footing for your dog and to prevent your sink or tub from being scratched.

Step Four: have everything you need for the bath (shampoo, conditioner, sponge, towels) right next to the sink or tub, so you don't have to go searching once your dog is already in the water. Place cotton balls in your Cavachon's ear canals to prevent accidental splashes from entering the ear canal.

Step Five: fill the tub or sink with four to six inches of lukewarm water (not too hot as dogs are more sensitive to hot water than us humans) and put your Cavachon in the water. Completely wet your dog's coat right down to the skin by using a detachable showerhead. If you don't have a spray attachment, a cup or pitcher will work just as well.

TIP: no dog likes to have water poured over its head and into its eyes, so use a wet sponge or wash cloth to wet the head area.

Step Six: apply shampoo as indicated on the bottle instructions by beginning at the head and working your way down the back. Be careful not to get shampoo in the eyes, nose, mouth or ears. Comb the shampoo lather through your dog's hair with your fingers, making sure you don't miss the areas under the legs and tail.

Step Seven: after allowing the shampoo to remain in your dog's coat for a couple of minutes, thoroughly rinse your Cavachon's coat right down to the skin with clean, lukewarm water using the spray attachment, cup or pitcher. Comb through your dog's coat with your fingers to make sure all shampoo residue has been rinsed away.

TIP: shampoo remaining in a dog's coat will lead to irritation and itching. Once you've rinsed, take the time to rinse again, especially in the armpits and underneath the tail area.

Use your hands to gently squeeze all excess water from your dog's coat.

Step Eight: apply conditioner as indicated on the bottle instructions and work the conditioner throughout your Cavachon's coat. Leave the conditioner in your dog's coat for two minutes and then thoroughly rinse the conditioner out of your dog's coat with warm water, unless the conditioner you are using is a "leave-in", no-rinse formula.

Pull the plug on your sink or tub and let the water drain away as you use your hands to squeeze excess water from your Cavachon's legs and feet.

Step Nine: immediately out of the water, wrap your Cavachon in dry towels so that they don't get cold and use the towels to gently squeeze out extra water before you allow them a water-spraying shake. If your dog has long hair, do not rub your dog with the towels, as this will create tangles and breakage in the long hair.

NOTE: if your dog has a short or shaved coat, you will not need to be so particular and in this case may massage the shampoo or conditioner in circular motions through the coat and can rub them down a little more with the towels after they are out of the tub.

Dry your Cavachon right away with your handheld hairdryer and be careful not to let the hot air get too close to their skin.

TIP: if your Cavachon's hair is longer, blow the hair in the direction of growth to help prevent breakage and if the hair is short, you can use your hand or a brush or comb to lift and fluff the hair to help it dry more quickly.

TIP: place your hand between the hairdryer and your Cavachon's hair so that they will never get a direct blast of hot air and never blow air directly into their face or ears.

Show Dog Coats

If you have decided to let your Cavachon keep a long, flowing coat that reaches the floor, be aware that this type of coat will need much higher maintenance.

Grooming can include weekly bathing and oiling of the coat to make the hair shine and to prevent hair from breaking and at the very least you will need to provide daily brushing and combing sessions to keep debris out of the longer hair.

Furthermore, you will need to be much more careful when bathing a Cavachon with a long, silky coat.

For instance, when you apply the shampoo onto the back, you will not want to rub in circles, but rather use only downward strokes to distribute the suds because washing up and down or massaging in circular motions will tangle and break the fine hair.

2. Clipping

If you have decided to learn how to clip your Cavachon's hair yourself, rather than taking them to a professional grooming salon, you will need to purchase all the tools necessary and learn how to properly use them.

The first step will be learning which blades to use in your electric clipper in order to get the length of cut you desire.

The "blade cut" refers to the length of the dog's hair that will remain after cutting against the natural line of the hair.

As an example, if the blade cut indicates 1/4" (0.6 cm) the length of your Cavachon's hair after cutting will be 1/4" (0.6 cm) if you cut with the natural growth of their hair, or it will be 1/8" (0.3 cm) if you cut against the direction of the hair growth.

Even if you decide to leave the full grooming to the professionals, in between grooming sessions you will still need to have a brush, a comb, a small pair of scissors and a pair of nail clippers on hand, so that you can keep the hair clipped away from your Cavachon's eyes, knots and tangles out of their coat and their nails trimmed short.

A good quality clipper for a Cavachon, such as an *"Andis"*, *"Wahl"* or *"Oster"* professional electric clipper will cost between $100 and $300 (£60 and £180) or more.

3. Ear Care

Your dog will also need it's ears clearing out occasional, as long-haired dogs like Cavachons can become very messy in the ear. A lot of people get very funny about this online, asking who would clean out their ears in the wild. The answer to that is that modern dogs aren't evolved to live in the wild and that they have been genetically engineered through hundreds of years of selective breeding programs. Your local pet store will offer a wide variety of ear cleaning creams, drops, oils, rinses, solutions and wipes specially formulated for cleaning your dog's ears.
In addition, there are also many home remedies that will just as efficiently clean your dog's ears.
Note: because a dog's ears are a very sensitive area, always read the labels before purchasing products and avoid any solutions that list alcohol as the main ingredient.

Some home ear cleaning solutions will be listed later on in this chapter.

4. Eye Care

Although some breeds, like the Cavachon, are much more prone to the build up of daily eye secretions, every dog should have their eyes regularly wiped with a warm, damp cloth to remove the build up of daily secretions in the corners of the eyes.

The Cavachon will be prone to a build up of secretions that can be unattractive and uncomfortable for the dog as the hair becomes glued together.

If this build up is not removed every day, it can quickly become a cause of bacterial yeast growth that can lead to eye infections.

When you take a moment every day to gently wipe your dog's eyes with a warm, moist cloth, and keep the hair trimmed away from their eyes, you will help to keep your dog's eyes comfortable and infection free.

5. Nail Care

Allowing your Cavachon to have long, untrimmed nails can result in various health hazards including infections or an irregular and uncomfortable gait that can result in damage to their skeleton.

Although most dogs do not particularly enjoy the process of having their nails trimmed, and most humans find the exercise to be a little scary, regular nail trimming is a very important grooming practice that should never be overlooked.

In order to keep your Cavachon's toenails in good condition and the proper length, you will need to purchase either a guillotine or plier nail trimmer at a pet store and learn how to correctly use it.

NOTE: when your Cavachon is a small puppy, it will be best to trim their nails with a pair of nail scissors, which you can purchase at any pet store, that are smaller and easier to use on smaller nails.

Furthermore, if you want your dog's nails to be smooth, without the sharp edges clipping alone can create, you will also want to invest in a toenail file or a special, slow speed rotary trimmer (Dremel™), designed especially for dog nails. Some dogs will prefer the rotary trimmer to the squeezing sensation of the nail clipper.

NOTE: never use a regular Dremel™ tool on a dog's toenails as it will be too high speed and will burn your dog's toenails. Only use a slow speed Dremel™, Model 7300-PT Pet Nail Grooming Tool.

6. Dental Care

As a conscientious Cavachon guardian you will need to regularly care for your dog's teeth throughout their entire life.

a) Retained Primary Teeth

Often a young dog will not naturally lose their puppy or baby teeth, especially those with small jaws, like the Cavachon, without intervention from a licensed veterinarian.

Therefore, keep a close watch on your puppy's teeth around the age of 6 or 7 months to make certain that the baby teeth have fallen out and that the adult teeth have space to grown in.

If your Cavachon puppy has not naturally lost their baby teeth, they will need to be pulled in order to allow room for the adult teeth to grow, and the best time to do this will be the same time they visit the veterinarian's office to be spayed or neutered.

Smaller dogs, like the Cavachon, have a smaller jaw, which can result in more problems with teeth overcrowding.

An overcrowded mouth can cause teeth to grow unevenly or crooked and food and plaque to build up, which will eventually result in bacterial growth on the surface of the teeth, causing bad breath, gum and dental disease.

b) Periodontal Disease

Please be aware that 80% of three-year-old dogs suffer from periodontal disease and bad breath because their guardians do not look after their dog's teeth.

What makes this shocking statistic even worse is that it is entirely possible to prevent canine gum disease and bad breath.

The pain associated with periodontal disease will make your dog's life miserable, as it will be painful for them to eat and the associated bacteria can infect many parts of the dog's body, including the heart, kidney, liver and brain, all of which they will have to suffer in silence.

If your Cavachon has bad breath, this could be the first sign of gum disease caused by plaque build-up on the teeth.

As well, if your Cavachon is drooling excessively, this may be a secondary symptom to dental disease. Your dog may be experiencing pain or the salivary glands may be reacting to inflammation from excessive bacteria in the mouth. If you notice your Cavachon drooling, you will want to have them professionally examined at your veterinarian's office.

c) Teeth Brushing

Slowly introduce your Cavachon to teeth brushing early on in their young life so that they will not fear it.

Begin with a finger cap toothbrush when they are young puppies, and then move to a soft-bristled toothbrush, or even an electric brush, as all you have to do is hold it against the teeth while the brush does all the work. Sometimes with a manual brush, you may brush too hard and cause the gums to bleed.

Never use human toothpaste or mouthwash on your dog's teeth because dogs cannot spit and human toothpaste that contains toxic fluoride will be swallowed. There are many flavoured dog toothpastes available at the pet store or veterinarian's office.

In addition, it is a good idea to get your dog used to the idea of occasionally having their teeth scraped or scaled, especially the back molars, which tend to build up plaque. Be very careful if you are doing this yourself because the tools are sharp.

TIP: if you need help keeping your dog's mouth open while you do a quick brush or scrape, get yourself a piece of hard material (rubber or leather) that they can bite down on, so that they cannot fully close their mouth while you work on their teeth.

Get your Cavachon used to having its mouth handled and your fingers rubbing their teeth and gums when they are a young puppy.

Next, buy some canine toothpaste at your local pet store specially flavoured to appeal to dogs and apply this to your dog's teeth with your finger.

Then slowly introduce the manual or electric toothbrush to your Cavachon. When you go slowly, they will get used to the buzzing of the electric brush, which will do a superior job of cleaning their teeth.

Firstly, let them see the electric brush, then let them hear it buzzing, and before you put it in their mouth, let them feel the buzzing sensation on their body, while you move it slowly toward their head and muzzle.

When your Cavachon will allow you to touch their muzzle while the brush is turned on, the next step is to brush a couple of teeth at a time until they get used to having them all brushed at the same time.

Whether you let the electric toothbrush do the work for you, or you are using a manual toothbrush, make sure that you brush in a circular motion with the bristles of the brush angled so that they get underneath the gum line to help prevent gum disease and loose teeth.

d) Teeth Scaling

The use of a tooth scraper once or twice a month can help to remove plaque build up. Most accumulation will be found on the outside of the teeth and on the back molars, near the gum line. Go slowly and carefully because these tools are sharp and only do this when your dog is calm and relaxed, a little bit at a time.

e) Healthy Teeth Tips

Despite what most dog owners might put up with as normal, it is not normal for your dog to have smelly dog breath or canine halitosis.

Bad breath is the first sign of an unhealthy mouth, which could involve gum disease or tooth decay.

The following tips will help keep your Cavachon's mouth and teeth healthy:

- Keep your dog's teeth sparkling white and their breath fresh by using old-fashioned hydrogen as your doggy toothpaste (hydrogen peroxide is what's in the human whitening toothpaste). There will be such a small amount on the brush that it will not harm your dog, and will kill any bacteria in your dog's mouth.

- Many canine toothpastes are formulated with active enzymes to help keep tartar build-up at bay.

- Help prevent tooth plaque and doggy halitosis by feeding your dog natural, hard bones at least once a month, which will also help to remove tartar while polishing and keeping their teeth white.

- Feed large bones so there is no danger of swallowing, and do NOT boil the bones first because this makes the bone soft (which defeats the purpose of removing plaque), and could cause it to splinter into smaller pieces that could create a choking hazard for your dog.

- Small dogs with shorter muzzles such as the Cavachon tend to be more vulnerable to teeth and gum problems; therefore, you really need to be brushing their teeth every single day.

- Feed them a daily dental chew or hard biscuit to help remove tartar whilst exercising the jaws and the massaging gums. Some dental chews contain natural breath freshening cinnamon, cloves or chlorophyll.

- Coconut oil also helps to prevent smelly dog breath while giving your dog's digestive, immune and metabolic functions a boost at the same time. Dogs love the taste, so add a 1/2 tsp to your Cavachon's dinner and their breath will soon be much sweeter.

Keep your Cavachon's mouth comfortable and healthy by getting into the habit of brushing their teeth every night before bedtime.

7. Skin Care

Keeping your Cavachon's coat clean free from debris and parasites by regularly bathing with canine shampoo and conditioner, as well as providing plenty of clean water and feeding them a high quality diet free from allergy-causing ingredients will go a long way towards keeping their skin healthy and itch-free.

8. Brushing and Combing

Brushing and combing your dog's coat is an often-overlooked task that is a necessary part of maintaining your dog's health.

As well, taking time to brush and comb your Cavachon's coat will also give you an opportunity to bond with your dog, while identifying any problems (such as lumps or bumps and matted hair) early on, before they may become more serious.

Make sure that your grooming sessions are as pleasant as possible by choosing the right tools for a Cavachon and their type and length of coat.

You will need a variety of brushes and combs to keep your Cavachon's coat in good condition, which will include a soft bristle brush, a slicker brush and a pin brush.

As well as your collection of brushes, you will need to invest in a metal comb, a flea comb and perhaps a mat splitter.

9. Equipment & Supplies Required

A **bristle brush** with its clusters of tightly packed bristles will remove loose hair, dirt and debris while gently stimulating the skin, improving circulation and adding shine to the coat.

A **pin brush** usually has an oval head with wire bristles that are individually spaced and embedded into a flexible rubber pad.

Most guardians prefer pin brushes with rubber tips as these help to prevent a wire from accidentally piercing a dog's sensitive skin.

A pin brush is more normally used following a thorough bristle brushing to lift and fluff the hair at the end of a grooming session.

A **slicker brush** has short, thin wire bristles arranged closely together and anchored to a flat, often rectangular surface that is attached to a handle.

A slicker brush is an ideal grooming tool for helping to remove mats and tangles from a Cavachon's coat. Slicker brushes are often used as a finishing brush after the use of a pin brush to smooth the dog's coat and create a shiny finish.

Mat Splitters, as the name suggests, are tools for splitting apart matted hair, and they come in three different types, including the letter opener style, the safety razor style and the curved blade style.

All of these tools are used to split matted fur into smaller, lengthwise pieces, with minimal discomfort to the dog, so that you or your groomer can untangle or shave the area with a clipper.

Combs are very useful for getting down to the base of any tangles in a dog's coat and working them loose before they develop into painful mats.

Most metal combs have a combination of widely spaced and narrow spaced teeth and are designed so that if you run into a tangle, you can switch to the wider spaced teeth while you work it out, without pulling and irritating your dog.

NOTE: Some combs have rotating teeth, which makes the process of removing tangles from your Cavachon's coat much easier on them without the pain of pulling and snagging.

Flea combs, as the name suggests, are designed for the specific purpose of removing fleas from a dog's coat.

A flea comb is usually small in size for manoeuvring in tight spaces, and may be made of plastic or metal with the teeth of the comb placed very close together, to trap hiding fleas.

In addition, you will want to keep a good quality pair of small **scissors** in your Cavachon grooming box, even if you do not want to do the full grooming process yourself, so that you can regularly trim around your Cavachon's eyes between full grooming sessions.

If you are planning on grooming your Cavachon yourself, you will need to invest in good quality scissors of several lengths that can cost anywhere between $30 and $200 each (£18 and £119) or more.

10. Products

a) Shampoos

NEVER make the mistake of using human shampoo or conditioner for bathing your Cavachon because dogs have a different pH balance than humans.

For example, shampoo for humans has a pH balance of 5.5, whereas shampoo formulated for our canine companions has an almost neutral pH balance of 7.5.

Any shampoo with a lower pH balance will be harmful to your dog because it will be too harshly acidic for their coat and skin, which can create skin problems.

Always purchase a shampoo for your dog that is specially formulated to be gentle and moisturizing on your Cavachon's coat and skin, that will not strip the natural oils, and that will nourish your dog's coat to give it a healthy shine.

As a general rule, always read the instructions provided on the shampoo bottle, and avoid shampoos containing insecticides or harsh chemicals.

Tip: if your Cavachon is suffering from an infestation of fleas, you may want to bathe them with shampoo containing pyrethrum (a botanical extract found in small, white daisies) or a shampoo containing citrus oil.

b) Conditioners

While many of us humans use a conditioner after we shampoo our own hair, a large number of us canine guardians forget to use a conditioner on our own dog's coat after bathing.

Even if the bathing process is one that you wish to complete as quickly as possible, you will want to reconsider this little oversight because, just as conditioning our human hair improves its condition, the same is true for our dog's coat.

Conditioning your Cavachon's coat will not only make it look and feel better, conditioning also has additional benefits, including:

- Preventing the escape of natural oils and moisture;
- Keeping the coat cleaner for a longer period of time;
- Repairing a coat that has become damaged or dry;
- Restoring a soft, silky feel;
- A conditioned coat will dry more quickly;
- Protection from the heat of the dryer and breakage from tangles during towelling, combing or brushing;

Spend the extra two minutes to condition your Cavachon's coat after bathing because the benefits of doing so will be appreciated by both you and your dog, which will have an overall healthy coat and skin with a natural shine.

c) De-tanglers

There are many de-tangling products that you can purchase that will make the job of combing and removing mats much easier on both you and your Cavachon, especially if you have opted to let their hair grow longer.

De-tangling products work by making the hair slippery, and while some de-tanglers work well when used full strength, you may prefer a lighter, spray-in product.

There are also silicone products and grooming powders, or you can even use corn starch to effectively lubricate the hair to help with removing mats and tangles before bathing.

d) Styptic Powder

You will always want to avoid causing any pain when trimming your Cavachon's toenails, because you don't want to destroy their trust in you regularly performing this task.

However, accidents do happen, therefore if you accidentally cut into the vein in the toenail, know that you will cause your dog pain, and the toenail will bleed.

Therefore, it is always a good idea to keep some styptic powder (often called "Kwik Stop") in your grooming kit. Dip a moistened finger into the powder and apply it immediately to the end of the bleeding nail.

The quickest way to stop a nail from bleeding is to immediately apply styptic powder and firm pressure for a few seconds.

Tip: if you do not have styptic powder or a styptic pencil available, there are several home remedies that can help stop the bleeding, including a mixture of baking soda and cornstarch, or simply cornstarch alone. Also, a cold, wet teabag or rubbing with scent-free soap can also be effective. These home remedies will not be as instantly effective as styptic powder.

e) Ear Powders

Ear powders, which can be purchased at any pet store, are designed to help keep your dog's ears dry while at the same time inhibiting the growth of bacteria that can lead to infections.

f) Ear Cleaning Solutions

Your local pet store will offer a wide variety of ear cleaning creams, drops, oils, rinses, solutions and wipes specially formulated for cleaning your dog's ears.

In addition, there are also many home remedies that will just as efficiently clean your dog's ears.

Note: because a dog's ears are a very sensitive area, always read the labels before purchasing products and avoid any solutions that list alcohol as the main ingredient.

g) Home Ear Cleaning Solutions

The following are three effective home solutions that will efficiently clean your dog's ears:

- **Witch Hazel** is a natural anti-inflammatory that works well to cleanse and protect against infection while encouraging faster healing of minor skin traumas.

- A 50:50 solution of **Organic Apple Cider Vinegar and Purified Water** has been used as an external folk medicine for decades. This mixture is a gentle and effective solution that kills germs while naturally healing.

- A 50:50 solution of **Hydrogen Peroxide and Purified Water** is useful for cleansing wounds and dissolving earwax.

Whatever product you decide to use for cleaning your dog's ears, always be careful about what you put into your dog's ears and thoroughly dry them after cleaning.

h) Canine Toothpastes

When it comes time to brush a dog's teeth, this is where many guardians fail miserably, using the excuse that *"my dog doesn't like it"*. Whether they like it or not is not the issue, because in order to keep your Cavachon healthy, they must have healthy teeth and the only way to ensure this is to brush their teeth every day.

The many canine types of toothpaste on the market are usually flavoured with beef or chicken in an attempt to appeal to the dog's taste buds, while others may be infused with mint or some other breath freshening ingredient in an attempt to appeal to humans by improving the dog's breath.

Honestly, your dog is not going to be begging for you to brush his or her teeth no matter how tasty the paste might be, therefore effectiveness, in the shortest period of time, will be more of a deciding factor than whether or not your dog prefers the taste of the toothpaste.

Some dog toothpastes contain baking soda, which is the same mild abrasive found in many human pastes, and is designed to gently scrub the teeth. However, just how much time you will have to spend scrubbing your dog's teeth, before they've had enough, may be too minimal to make these pastes very effective.

Other types of canine toothpastes are formulated with enzymes that are designed to work chemically by breaking down tartar or plaque in the dog's mouth. These pastes do not need to be washed off your dog's teeth and are safe for them to swallow. Whether or not they remain on the dog's teeth long enough to do any good might be debatable.

Tip: old-fashioned hydrogen peroxide cleans while killing germs and keeping teeth white. Just dip your dog's toothbrush in a capful of hydrogen peroxide, shake off the excess, and brush their teeth. There will such a small amount in your dog's mouth that you don't need to worry about them swallowing it.

i) Paw Creams

Depending upon the types of surfaces our canine counterparts usually walk on, they may suffer from cracked or rough pads.

You can restore resiliency and keep your Cavachon's paws in healthy condition by regularly applying a cream or lotion to protect their paw pads.

TIP: a good time to do this is just after you have clipped their nails.

11. Professional Grooming

If you decide that you are not interested in buying all the equipment (electric clippers, blades, scissors, nail clippers, combs, brushes, table, etc.) or enrolling yourself in a $4,000 (£2,388) course to learn how to professionally groom your Cavachon yourself, you will want to locate a trusted professional service to do this for you.

The best way to find a groomer is to ask others who they use and whether they are happy with the results.

If you have decided to keep your Cavachon clipped short in a puppy cut, you will need to take them for a full grooming session approximately every 6 to 8 weeks.

An average price for professionally grooming a small Cavachon will usually start around $40 (£24) and could be considerably more depending upon whether the salon is also bathing and trimming nails.

Chapter 6) Feeding your dog

The long-term health and wellbeing of your Cavachon is closely related to their nutrition. In fact, it's partly reliant on their diet.

Dogs are not, as is commonly believed, carnivores. In the wild they will eat animals that they've killed or found, graze on grass and help themselves to any fruit and nuts that they can reach.

A small dog like a Cavachon should be fed a large handful of dry food after the morning walk to nibble on during the day, a third to a half a tin of wet food after the afternoon walk and water all day. IT IS AGAINST THE LAW not to provide adequate food and water. It's horrifically bad for your dog's physical and mental health not to have a food routine too. Your dog needs a good, healthy diet to help keep them fit and healthy. Young puppies are going to grow at a phenomenal rate, taking up lots of energy and using lots of vitamins and minerals to make bones and lots of protein to build muscles. There are some great puppy formula foods out there and they should be fed on puppy food for the first 9 months to year of their life.

For the best, healthiest option you should give a combination of wet and dry food. Dry food can be left down all day, but if your dog gets overweight, you should take it up after half an hour to avoid constant browsing. Wet food should not be left down for more than half an hour, and the dog will soon learn that they should eat all they want in that time.

Meal times for your dog should be after your meal times 2-3 times a day. As your dog gets very old they will need smaller meals more often.

YOUR DOG SHOULD ALWAYS HAVE ACCES TO WATER. Not only is it stupid and dangerous not to allow your dog access to water all day, it is against the law. Not providing sufficient water is a crime that is punishable by a fine or time in prison. Not only this, but a lack of sufficient water can cause all sorts of long-term health problems.

1. Feeding Puppies

For growing puppies, a general feeding rule of thumb is to feed 10% of the puppy's present body weight or between 2% and 3% of their projected adult weight each day.

Keep in mind that high-energy puppies will require extra protein to help them to grow and develop into healthy adult dogs, especially during their first two years of life.

There are now many foods on the market that are formulated for all stages of a dog's life (including the puppy stage), so whether you choose one of these foods or a food specially formulated for puppies, they will need to be fed smaller meals more frequently throughout the day (3 or 4 times) until they are at least one year of age.

NOTE: choose quality sources of meat protein for healthy puppies and dogs, including beef, buffalo, chicken, duck, fish, hare, lamb, ostrich, pork, rabbit, turkey, venison, or any other source of wild, meaty protein.

2. Feeding Adults

An adult dog will generally need to be fed 2 to 3% of their body weight each day. Read the labels and avoid foods that contain a high amount of grains and other fillers. Choose foods that list high quality meat protein as the main ingredient.

TIP: grated parmesan cheese sprinkled on a Cavachon's dinner will help to stop picky eaters from ignoring their food.

3. Treats

Since the creation of the first dog treat over 150 years ago, the myriad of choices available on every pet store, feed store and grocery store shelf almost outnumbers those looking forward to eating them.

Today's treats are not just for making us guilty humans feel better because it makes us happy to give our fur friends something they really like; today's treats are designed to improve our dog's health.

Some of us humans treat our dogs just because, others use treats for training purposes, others for health, while still others treat for a combination of reasons.

Whatever reason you choose to give treats to your Cavachon, keep in mind that if we treat our dogs too often throughout the day, we may create a picky eater who will no longer want to eat their regular meals.
Furthermore, if the treats we are giving are high calorie, we may be putting our dog's health in jeopardy by allowing them to become overweight.

Carrots make a fantastic, sweet tasting treat that also helps to clean teeth. Carrots are full of vitamins and goodness. I can't stress enough how good carrots are!

Bones from the pet shop or the butchers are fantastic for little dogs. They give something to concentrate on. They are a good distraction from chewing furniture and other unwanted chewing behaviours. Beef knuckles are the best. Cooked chicken bones are a big no-no, as they can splinter and hurt the throat and stomach.

Cooked pumpkin is a good, sweet treat for your dog. It helps to recover from diarrhoea *and* constipation.

Banana is a great treat. It's high in potassium, it's sweet, it's soft, and it has a strong, delicious smell so they can use their nose to find it. Bananas are a fantastic treat for training. It also prevents eating poop.

Loaded with protein and a host of vitamins and minerals, eggs provide all sorts of proteins that are good for the skin and coat.

4. Treats to Avoid

a) Rawhide

Rawhide is soaked in an ash/lye solution to remove every particle of meat, fat and hair and then further soaked in bleach to remove remaining traces of the ash/lye solution. Now that the product is no longer food, it no longer has to comply with food regulations.

While the hide is still wet it is shaped into rawhide chews, and upon drying, it shrinks to approximately 1/4 of its original size.

Furthermore, arsenic-based products are often used as preservatives, and antibiotics and insecticides are added to kill bacteria that also fight against good bacteria in your dog's intestines.

The collagen fibres in the rawhide make it very tough and long-lasting, which makes this chew a popular choice for humans to give to their dogs because it satisfies the dog's natural urge to chew while providing many hours of quiet entertainment.

Sadly, when a dog chews on a rawhide treat, they ingest many harsh chemicals and when your dog swallows a piece of rawhide, that piece can swell up to four times its size inside your dog's stomach, which can cause anything from mild to severe gastric blockages that could become life threatening and require surgery.

b) Pig's Ears

These treats are actually the ears of pigs, and while most dogs will eagerly devour them, they are extremely high in fat, which can cause stomach upsets, vomiting and diarrhoea for many dogs.

Pig's ears are often processed and preserved with unhealthy chemicals that discerning dog guardians will not want to feed their dogs. While pig's ears are generally not considered to be a healthy treat choice for any dog, they should be especially avoided for any dog that may be at risk of being overweight.

c) Hoof Treats

Many humans give cow, horse and pig hooves to their dogs as treats because they consider them to be *"natural"*.

The truth is that after processing these *"treats"* they retain little, if any, of their *"natural"* qualities.

Hoof treats are processed with preservatives, including insecticides, lead, bleach, arsenic based products, and antibiotics to kill bacteria, which can also harm the good bacteria in your dog's intestines, and if all bacteria is not killed in these meat-based products before feeding them to your dog, they could also suffer from Salmonella poisoning.

Hooves can also cause the chipping or breaking of your dog's teeth as well as perforation or blockages in your dog's intestines.

d) Other food that is not good for your dog.

Onions and garlic can kill your dog. A big load of onions or garlic in one sitting or a small amount as little as once a week can break down the red blood cells, causing anaemia and eventual cell death in the muscles. Because of the small size of Cavachons, the risk with onions and garlic is much larger than with other breeds, as their size means they have more blood, so a little damage can be absorbed into the daily wear and tear and be repaired quicker. A lot of raw feeding websites and recipes suggest garlic to flavour food for your dog. While garlic is delicious, it can kill your dog. Anti-freeze is sweet but we don't drink it because it can kill us, so the same should go for garlic and dogs.

Chocolate is toxic. Even to humans, although the lethal dose couldn't really be consumed in one sitting for people. For dogs, though, the amount needed to do serious damage is much lower. The dangerous chemical in chocolate is theobromine. The problem a lot of people don't realise is that it's also in white chocolate. Theobromine can cause vomiting, diarrhoea, and be excessive thirst, abnormal heart rhythm, tremors, seizures, and death. Best not to risk it, eh?

Citrus fruits of all types can cause acidity problems in your dog's stomach. This can lead to vomiting, diarrhoea and general upset stomachs.

Grapes and raisins can cause kidney failure in dogs. The exact cause isn't known, but grapes and raisins, though delicious, are best avoided. They can make them incredibly ill. If they've pinched one off the coffee table then you're probably ok, but they shouldn't have them as a treat.

Avocados contain a substance called persin. Persin is fine for humans but for dogs it can cause all sorts of problems if eaten in large quantities. It is an oil-soluble acid that is good for people (unless you're allergic!) Too much persin can cause vomiting, constipation or diarrhoea. Not pleasant.

When your dog is young they will need a specific puppy food, then an adult food then a senior food. Always aim to feed a combination of "complete" dog foods, along with healthy treats.

Fresh, clean, raw meat would be a perfect source of quality protein for your dog. However—and this is a big however—the meat most of us have access to just isn't pristine. Salmonella is a major concern, especially in raw poultry (not to mention the danger posed by chicken bones), and all raw meat carries the risk of microbes and parasites, including E. coli. While many do feed their dogs raw meat to no ill effect, some dogs get very sick. If you do decide to raw feed this route (and you will not be alone, as the raw movement is gaining more and more adherents), be sure your ingredients are absolutely fresh, watch out for bones, and keep a close eye on your dog's complete needs. If you feed meat, then you should also feed grains. Half a cup of cooked rice is very good for your dog, especially if they aren't having commercial pet food.

Commercial pet food companies have put decades of research and hundreds of thousands into dog nutrition. It isn't lazy to feed bought pet food. It isn't bad for your dog to eat bought pet food. Just make sure you offer a variety of complete foods, healthy treats and supplements.

5. Healthy Treats

a) Hard Treats

There are so many choices of hard or crunchy treats available that come in many varieties of shapes, sizes and flavours, that you may have a difficult time choosing. If your Cavachon will eat them, hard treats will help to keep their teeth cleaner.

Whatever you choose, read the labels and make sure that the ingredients are high quality and appropriately sized for your Cavachon friend.

b) Soft Treats

Soft, chewy treats are also available in a wide variety of flavours, shapes and sizes for all the different needs of our furry friends and are often used for training purposes as they have a stronger smell.

Often smaller dogs, such as the Cavachon, prefer the soft, chewy treats to the hard crunchy ones.

c) Dental Treats

Dental treats or chews are designed with the specific purpose of helping your Cavachon to maintain healthy teeth and gums. They usually require intensive chewing and are often shaped with high ridges and bumps to exercise the jaw and massage gums while removing plaque build-up near the gum line.

d) Freeze-Dried and Jerky Treats

Freeze-dried and jerky treats offer a tasty morsel most dogs find irresistible as they are usually made of simple, meaty ingredients, such as liver, poultry and seafood. These treats are usually lightweight and easy to carry around, which means they can also be great as training treats.

e) Human Food Treats

You will want to be very careful when feeding human foods to dogs as treats, because many of our foods contain additives and ingredients that could be toxic and harmful.

Be certain to choose simple, fresh foods with minimal or no processing, such as lean meat, poultry or seafood, and even if your Cavachon will eat anything put in front of them, be aware that many common human foods, such as grapes, raisins, onions and chocolate are poisonous to dogs.

f) Training Treats

While any sort of treat can be used as an extra incentive during training sessions, soft treats are often used for training purposes because of their stronger smell and smaller sizes.

Yes, we humans love to treat our dogs, whether for helping to teach the new puppy to go pee outside, teaching the adolescent dog new commands, for trick training, for general good behaviour, or for no reason at all, other than that they just gave us the *"look"*.

Make sure the treats you choose are high quality, so that you can help to keep your Cavachon both happy and healthy, and generally, the treats you feed should not make up more than approximately 10% of their daily food intake.

6. Choosing the Right Food

From the meagre beginning of the first commercially made dog food has sprung a massively lucrative and vastly confusing industry that has only recently begun to evolve beyond those early days of feeding our dogs the dregs of human leftovers because it was cheap and convenient for us.

Even today, the majority of dog food choices have far more to do with being convenient for us humans to serve than it does with being a diet truly designed to be a well balanced, healthy food choice for a canine.

The dog food industry is big business and as such, because there are now almost limitless choices, there is much confusion and endless debate when it comes to answering the question, *"What is the best food for my dog?"*

Educating yourself by talking to experts and reading everything you can find on the subject, plus taking into consideration several relevant factors, will help to answer the dog food question.

For instance, where you live may dictate what sorts of foods you have access to. Other factors to consider will include the particular requirements of your dog, such as their age, energy and activity levels.

Next will be expense, time and quality. While we all want to give our dogs the best food possible, many humans lead very busy lives and cannot, for instance, prepare their own dog food, but still want to feed a high quality diet that fits within their budget.

However, perhaps most important when choosing an appropriate diet for our dogs is learning to be more observant of Mother Nature's design and taking a closer look at our dog's teeth, jaws and digestive tract.

While humans are herbivores who derive energy from eating plants, our canine companions are carnivores, which means they derive their energy and nutrient requirements from eating a diet consisting mainly or exclusively of flesh or animal tissues (i.e. meat).

a) The Canine Teeth

The first part of your dog that you will want to take a good look at when considering what to feed them will be their teeth.

Unlike humans, who are equipped with wide, flat molars for grinding grains, vegetables and other plant-based materials, canine teeth are all pointed because they are designed to rip, shred and tear into animal meat and bone.

b) The Canine Jaw

Another obvious consideration when choosing an appropriate food source for our fur friends is the fact that every canine is born equipped with powerful jaws and neck muscles for the specific purpose of being able to pull down and tear apart their hunted prey.

The structure of the jaw of every canine is such that it opens widely to hold large pieces of meat and bone, while the mechanics of a dog's jaw permits only vertical (up and down) movement that is designed for crushing.

c) The Canine Digestive Tract

A dog's digestive tract is short and simple and designed to move their natural choice of food (hide, meat and bone) quickly through their systems.

Vegetables and plant matter require more time to break down in the gastrointestinal tract, which in turn requires a more complex digestive system than the canine body is equipped with.

The canine digestive system is simply unable to break down vegetable matter, which is why whole vegetables look pretty much the same going into your dog as they do coming out the other end.

Given the choice, most dogs would never choose to eat plants or vegetables and fruits over meat; however, we humans continue to feed them a kibble-based diet that contains high amounts of vegetables and grains and low amounts of meat.

Plus, in order to get our dogs to eat fruits, vegetables and grains we usually have to flavour the food with meat or meat by-products.

How much healthier and long lived might our beloved fur friends be if, instead of largely ignoring nature's design for our canine companions, we chose to feed them whole, unprocessed, species-appropriate food?

With many hundreds of dog food brands to choose from, it's no wonder we humans are confused about what to feed our dogs to help them live long and healthy lives.

Below are some suggestions and questions that may help you to choose a dog food company that you can feel comfortable with:

- How long have they been in business?
- Is dog food their main industry?
- Are they dedicated to their brand?
- Are they easily accessible?
- If you contact them, do they honestly answer your questions?
- Research the Company's Safety Standard
- Look for pet food companies that set higher standards
- Read the ingredients - where did they come from?
- Are the ingredients something you would eat?
- Are the ingredients farmed locally?
- Was it cooked in a kitchen using standards you would trust?
- Is the company certified under human food or organic guidelines?

Whatever you decide to feed your Cavachon, keep in mind that, just as too much wheat, other grains and other fillers in our human diet is having detrimental effects on our health, the same can be very true for our dogs.

Our dogs are also suffering from many of the same life threatening diseases that are rampant in our human society as a direct result of consuming a diet high in genetically altered, impure, processed and packaged foods.

7. The Raw Diet

While some of us believe that we are killing ourselves as well as our dogs with processed foods, others believe that there are dangers in feeding raw foods.

Those who are raw feeding advocates believe that the ideal diet for their dog is one which would be very similar to what a dog living in the wild would have access to, and these canine guardians are often opposed to feeding their dog any sort of commercially manufactured pet foods, because they consider them to be poor substitutes.

On the other hand, those opposed to feeding their dogs a raw or biologically appropriate raw food diet believe that the risks associated with food-borne illnesses during the handling and feeding of raw meats outweigh the purported benefits.

Interestingly, even though the United States Food and Drug Administration (FDA) states that they do not advocate a raw diet for dogs, they do advise that for those who wish to take this route, following basic hygiene guidelines for handling raw meat can minimize any associated risks.

Furthermore, high pressure pasteurization (HPP), which is high pressure, water based technology for killing bacterium, is USDA-approved for use on organic and natural food products, and is being utilized by many commercial raw pet food manufacturers.

Raw meats purchased at your local grocery store contain a much higher level of acceptable bacteria than raw food produced for dogs because the meat purchased for human consumption is meant to be cooked, which will kill any bacteria that might be present.

This means that canine guardians feeding their dogs a raw food diet can be quite certain that commercially prepared raw foods sold in pet stores will be safer than raw meats purchased in grocery stores.

Many guardians of high energy, working breed dogs will agree that their dogs thrive on a raw or BARF (Biologically

Appropriate Raw Food) diet and strongly believe that the potential benefits of feeding a raw dog food diet are many, including:

- Healthy, shiny coats
- Decreased shedding
- Fewer allergy problems
- Healthier skin
- Cleaner teeth
- Fresher breath
- Higher energy levels
- Improved digestion
- Smaller stools
- Strengthened immune system
- Increased mobility in arthritic pets
- General increase or improvement in overall health

All dogs, whether working breeds or lap dogs, are amazing athletes in their own right; therefore every dog deserves to be fed the best food available.

A raw diet is a direct evolution of what dogs ate before they became our domesticated pets and we turned towards commercially prepared, easy to serve dry dog food that required no special storage or preparation.

The BARF diet is all about feeding our dogs what they are designed to eat by returning them to their evolutionary diet.

When considering the health of your Cavachon, it is certainly worth remembering that just as too much wheat and processed foods in our human diet is having detrimental effects on our health, the same can be very true for our best fur friends who are also suffering from many of the same life threatening diseases that are rampant in our society today.

8. The Dehydrated Diet

Dehydrated dog food comes in both raw and cooked forms and these foods are usually air dried to reduce moisture to the level where bacterial growths are inhibited.

The appearance of de-hydrated dog food is very similar to dry kibble and the typical feeding methods include adding warm water before serving, which makes this type of diet both healthy for our dogs and convenient for us to serve.

Dehydrated recipes are made from minimally processed fresh whole foods to create a healthy and nutritionally balanced meal that will meet or exceed the dietary requirements for healthy canines.

Dehydrating removes only the moisture from the fresh ingredients, which usually means that because the food has not already been cooked at a high temperature, more of the overall nutrition is retained.

A de-hydrated diet is a convenient way to feed your dog a nutritious diet because all you have to do is add warm water, and wait five minutes while the food re-hydrates so your Cavachon can enjoy a warm meal.

9. The Kibble Diet

While many canine guardians are starting to take a closer look at the food choices they are making for their furry companions, there is no mistaking that the convenience and relative economy of dry dog food kibble, that had its beginnings in the 1940's, continues to be the most popular pet food choice for most dog-friendly humans.

Some 75 years later, the massive pet food industry offers up a confusingly large number of choices with hundreds of different manufacturers and brand names lining the shelves of veterinarian offices, grocery stores and pet food aisles.

While feeding a high quality, bagged kibble diet that has been flavoured to appeal to dogs and supplemented with vegetables and fruits to appeal to humans may keep almost every Cavachon companion happy and healthy, you will need to decide whether this is the best diet for them.

10. The Right Bowl

Here is a brief description of the different categories and types of dog bowls that would be appropriate choices for your Cavachon's particular needs:

Automatic Watering Bowls: are standard dog bowls (often made out of plastic) that are attached to a reservoir container, which is designed to keep water constantly available to your dog as long as there is water remaining in the storage compartment.

Ceramic/Stoneware Bowls: are a great choice for those who like options in personality, colour and shape.

Elevated Bowls: raised dining table dog bowls are a tidy and classy choice that will make your dog's dinner time a more comfortable experience while getting the bowls off the floor.

Non-Skid Bowls: are for dogs that push their bowls across the floor when eating. A non-skid dog bowl will help keep the feed bowl where you put it.

No Tip Bowls: are designed to prevent the messy type of doggy eater from flipping over their dinner or water bowls.

Stainless Steel Bowls: are as close to indestructible as a bowl can be, plus they are sanitary and easy to clean and water stays cooler for a longer period of time in a stainless bowl.

Wooden Bowls: for those humans concerned about stylish home decor, wooden dog bowl dining stations are beautiful pieces of furniture unto themselves that can enhance your home decor.

Travel Bowls: are convenient, practical and handy additions to the travelling canine. Instead of a cloth bowl that is difficult to clean, consider a space saving, collapsible dog bowl, made out of hygienic, renewable bamboo that comes in fun colours and different sizes, making it perfect for every travel bowl need.

If you would like to learn more about all the many dog bowl choices available, visit DogBowlForYourDog.com, which is a comprehensive, one-stop website dedicated to explaining the ins and outs of every food bowl imaginable and helping you find the perfect bowl for all your Cavachon's needs.

11. Supplements

It's a good idea to also give cod liver oil. A cod liver oil capsule every other day will just give extra oils for long-term joint health and condition. The long-term benefits of regular cod liver oil aren't dramatic; however it is proven to aid absorption of calcium to maintain strong healthy bones.

Added calcium is bad for a dog. Don't give calcium unless your vet instructs it.

Vitamin A can seriously damage the blood vessels and should only be given if your vet advises it.

Vitamin D can make your dog loose muscle tone.

Chapter 7) House training

1. Human Training

House training, or "potty" training, is a critical first step in the education of any new puppy, and the first part of a successful process is training the human guardian.

When you bring home your new Cavachon puppy, they will be relying upon your guidance to teach them what they need to learn.

When you provide your puppy with your consistent patience and understanding, they are capable of learning rules at a very early age, and house training is no different, especially since it's all about establishing a regular routine.

Potty training a new puppy takes time and patience — how much time depends entirely upon you.

Check in with yourself and make sure your energy remains consistently calm and patient and that you exercise plenty of compassion and understanding while you help your new puppy learn the new bathroom rules.

Cavachon puppies and dogs flourish with routines and so do humans, therefore, the first step is to establish a daily routine that will work well for both canine and human alike.

For instance, depending upon the age of your Cavachon puppy, make a plan to take them out for a bathroom break every two hours and stick to it because while you are in the beginning stages of potty training, the more vigilant and consistent you can be, the quicker and more successful your results will be.

Generally speaking, while your puppy is still growing, a young puppy can hold it approximately one hour for every month of their age.

This means that if your 2-month-old puppy has been happily snoozing for a couple of hours, as soon as they wake up, they will need to go outside.

Some of the first indications or signs that your puppy needs to be taken outside to relieve themselves will be when you see them:

- Sniffing around
- Circling
- Looking for the door
- Whining, crying or barking
- Acting agitated

It will be important to always take your Cavachon puppy out first thing every morning, and immediately after they wake up from a nap as well as soon after they have finished eating a meal or having a big drink of water.

Also, your happy praise goes a long way towards encouraging and reinforcing future success when your Cavachon puppy makes the right decisions, so let them know you are happy when they do their business in the right place.

Initially, treats can be a good way to reinforce how happy you are that your puppy is learning to relieve themselves in the right place. Slowly, treats can be removed and replaced with your happy praise.

Next, now that you have a new puppy in your life, you will want to be flexible with respect to adapting your schedule to meet the requirements that will help to quickly teach your Cavachon puppy their new bathroom routine.

This means not leaving your puppy alone for endless hours at a time because firstly, they are pack animals that need companionship and your direction at all times, plus long periods alone will result in the disruption of the potty training schedule you have worked hard to establish.

If you have no choice but to leave your puppy alone for many hours, make sure that you place them in a paper-lined room or pen where they can relieve themselves without destroying your favourite carpet.

Remember, your Cavachon is a growing puppy with a bladder and bowels that they do not yet have complete control over and you will have a much happier time and better success if you simply train yourself to pay attention to when your young companion is showing signs of needing to relieve themselves.

DO NOT LEAVE YOUR DOG IN THEIR OWN FILTH. Not only is this cruel, it's illegal. Puppies can't hold it for as long as older dogs can, and untrained dogs don't know that they're supposed to hold it. Dogs naturally avoid fouling in their home, so early house training is about presenting as many opportunities to do their business. Dogs need a regular routine anyway, and being walked or let out 4 or more times a day to pee and poop, you can build this into the routine. Knowing roughly how long they have to hold on between time outdoors really helps to speed up toilet training. As with everything you're training your dog to do, reward wanted behaviour. When your little Cavachon does it's business outdoors or on the paper/ puppy pads – give them a fuss. Happy voice, "good girl!" scruffle their head and show them you're pleased with them for going in the right place. Until the dog is about 6-8 months old there will be accidents. They can't help it – they are babies without nappies on. Do not react to messes on the floor – this teaches the dog how to make you cross. Instead, you should clean the mess as quickly and as thoroughly as possible. A dog takes a lot of cues from smell. The smell of urine is a mark that stays and suggests that this is where we pee.

Toilet instructions are, once again, quite easy. Choose your word. In most cases, people say "make". Every time you are outside and the dog is doing their business say the command and reward the dog. Then try to say it just before the dog goes, try to recognize the signs of when your dog is getting ready and say the command word. Once the dog has done its business after you have 'told' it to, reward the dog. Try to do this in the same place each time. Eventually the sound of the word will make the dog want to relieve itself as soon as possible and you will have trained your dog to 'go' when you want it to.

The best routine for letting your dog go when they need to is to walk – or be let out – first thing in the morning, as soon as you get in from work or between 4 and 6 if you're about all day, and one last walk or toilet break last thing before bed.

2. Bell Training

A very easy way to introduce your new Cavachon puppy to house training is to begin by teaching them how to ring a doorbell whenever they need to go outside.

Ringing a doorbell is not only a convenient alert system for both you and your Cavachon puppy or dog, but your visitors will be most impressed by how smart your Cavachon is.

A further benefit of training your puppy to ring a bell is that you will not have to listen to your puppy or dog whining, barking or howling to be let out, and your door will not become scratched up from their nails.

Unless you prefer to purchase an already manufactured doggy doorbell or system, take a trip to your local novelty store and purchase a small bell that has a nice, loud ring.

Attach the bell to a piece of ribbon or string and hang it from a door handle or tape it to a doorsill near the door where you will be taking your puppy out when they need to relieve themselves. The string will need to be long enough so that your Cavachon puppy can easily reach the bell with their nose or a paw.

Next, each time you take your puppy out to relieve themselves, say the word *"Out"*, and use their paw or their nose to ring the bell. Praise them for this "trick" and immediately take them outside.

The only down side to teaching your Cavachon puppy or dog to ring a bell when they want to go outside is that even if they don't actually have to go out to relieve themselves, but just want to go outside because they are bored, you will still have to take them out every time they ring the bell.

There are many types and styles of *"gotta' go"* commercially manufactured bells you could choose from, ranging from the elegant **"Poochie Bells™"** that hang from a doorknob, the simple **"Tell Bell™"** that sits on the floor, or various high-tech door chime systems that function much like a doggy intercom system where they push a pad with their paw and it rings a bell.

Whatever doorbell system you choose for your Cavachon puppy, once they are trained, this type of alert system is an easy way to eliminate accidents in the home.

3. Kennel Training

Kennel training is always a good idea for any puppy early in their education because it can be utilized for many different situations, including being a very helpful tool for house training.

When purchasing a kennel for your Cavachon puppy, always buy a kennel that will be the correct size for your Cavachon puppy once they become adult size. The kennel will be the correct size if your fully grown Cavachon dog can stand up and easily turn around inside their kennel.

When you train your Cavachon puppy to accept sleeping in their own kennel at night time, this will also help to accelerate their potty training, because no puppy or dog wants to relieve themselves where they sleep, which means that they will hold their bladder and bowels as long as they possibly can.

4. Exercise Pen Training

The exercise pen is a transition from kennel-only training and will be helpful for those times when you may have to leave your Cavachon puppy for more hours than they can reasonably be expected to hold it.

During those times when you must be away from the home for several hours, it's time to introduce your Cavachon puppy to an exercise pen.

Exercise pens are usually constructed of wire sections that you can put together in whatever shape you desire, and the pen needs to be large enough to hold your puppy's kennel on one half of the pen, while the other half will be lined with newspapers or pee pads.

Place your Cavachon puppy's food and water dishes next to the kennel and leave the kennel door open so they can wander in and out whenever they wish, to eat or drink or go to the papers if they need to relieve themselves.

Your puppy will be contained in a small area of your home while you are away and because they are already used to sleeping inside their kennel, they will not want to relieve themselves inside the area where they sleep. Therefore, your Cavachon puppy will naturally go to the other half of the pen to relieve themselves on the newspapers or pee pads.

This method will help train your puppy to be quickly paper-trained when you have to be away for a few hours.

5. Puppy Apartment™ Training

While a similar concept and a more costly alternative, the *Puppy Apartment*™ is a step up from the exercise pen training system that makes the process of crate or pen training even easier on both humans and puppies.

The Puppy Apartment™ works well in a variety of situations, whether you're at home and unable to pay close attention to your Cavachon puppy's needs, whether you must be away from the home for a few hours or during the evening when everyone is asleep and you don't particularly want to get up at 3:00 a.m. to take your Cavachon puppy out to go pee. The Puppy Apartment™ is an innovation that is convenient for both puppy and human alike.

What makes this system so effective is the patent, pending dividing wall with a door leading to the other side, all inside the pen. One side of the Puppy Apartment™ is where the puppy's bed is located and the other side (through the doorway) is the bathroom area that is lined with pee pads.

With the bathroom right next door, your Cavachon puppy or dog can relieve themselves whenever they wish, without the need to alert family members to let them out.

This one bedroom, one bathroom system, which is a combination of the kennel/training pen, is a great alternative for helping to eliminate the stress of worrying about always keeping a watchful eye on your puppy or getting up in the night to take them outside every few hours to help them avoid making mistakes.

According to *"Modern Puppies"*...

> *"The Puppy Apartment™ takes the MESSY out of paper training, the ODORS AND HASSLES out of artificial grass training, MISSING THE MARK out of potty pad training and HAVING TO HOLD IT out of crate training. House training a puppy has never been faster or easier!*
>
> *The Puppy Apartment™ has taken all the benefits of the most popular potty training methods and combined them into one magical device and potty training system. This device and system has revolutionized how modern puppies are potty trained!"*

Manufactured in the United States, this product ships directly from the California supplier (Modern Puppies).

The price of the Puppy Apartment™ begins at $138. USD (£83.37) and is only available online at Modern Puppies.

6. Free Training

If you would rather not confine your young Cavachon puppy to one or two rooms in your home, and will be allowing them to freely range about your home anywhere they wish during the day. This is considered free training.

When free house training your Cavachon puppy, you will need to closely watch your puppy's activities all day long so that you can be aware of the *"signs"* that will indicate when they need to go outside to relieve themselves.

For instance, circling and sniffing is a sure sign that they are looking for a place to do their business.

Never get upset or scold a puppy for having an accident inside the home, because this will result in teaching your puppy to be afraid of you and to only relieve themselves in secret places or when you're not watching.

If you catch your Cavachon puppy making a mistake, all that is necessary is for you to calmly say *"No"*, and quickly scoop them up and take them outside or to their indoor bathroom area. From your puppy's point of view, yelling or screaming when they make a potty mistake is unstable energy being displayed by the person who is supposed to be their leader and this type of behaviour will only teach your puppy to fear and disrespect you.

The Cavachon is not a difficult puppy to housebreak and they will generally do very well when you start them off with *"puppy pee pads"* that you will move closer and closer to the same door that you always use when taking them outside. This way they will quickly learn to associate going to this door when they need to relieve themselves.

When you pay close attention to your Cavachon puppy's sleeping, eating, drinking and playing habits, you will quickly learn their body language so that you are able to predict when they might need to relieve themselves.

Your Cavachon puppy will always need to relieve themselves first thing in the morning, as soon as they wake up from a nap, approximately 20 minutes after they finish eating a meal, after they have finished a play session, and of course, before they go to bed at night.

It's important to have compassion during this house training time in your young Cavachon's life so that their education will be as stress-free as possible.

It's also important to be vigilant because how well you pay attention will minimize the opportunities your puppy may have for making a bathroom mistake in the first place, and the fewer mistakes they make, the sooner your Cavachon puppy will be house trained.

7. Professional Cleaning Products

Remember that a dog's sense of smell is at least 2,000 times more sensitive that our human sense of smell.

As a result of your Cavachon puppy's superior sense of smell, it will be very important to effectively remove all odours from house training accidents, because otherwise your Cavachon puppy will be attracted by the smell to the place where they may have had a previous accident, and will want to do their business there again and again.

While there are many products that are supposed to remove odours and stains, many of these are not very effective. You want a professional grade cleaner that will not just mask one odour with another scent, but that will completely neutralize odours.

TIP: go to RemoveUrineOdors.com and order yourself some *"SUN"* and/or *"Max Enzyme"* because these products contain professional-strength odour neutralizers and urine digesters that bind to and completely absorb odours on any type of surface.

Chapter 8) Training and behaviour

Where your dog comes from can make a real difference to its behaviour and ability to be trained. Dogs that are not socialized well at a young age do not make great pets, but you can sometimes, with a massive amount of time and effort, fix them if you've already bought a "bad puppy". Sometimes you will find yourself with a rescue dog that was not exactly as he was labelled. Now you have a bad dog. The heartbreaking decision to take the dog back to the dog's home or the pound is sometimes the right one. Harsh as this may seem, an unpredictable dog with a family who can't fix it can be a tragedy waiting to happen, as well as a stressful and unhappy situation for both the dog and the owner. If you have the time, patience and discipline, however, a dog like this can sometimes be saved.

A well-trained dog is a happy dog. They know exactly what's expected of them and how to behave. They feel safe and secure. That is what they need from you the most. Having a dog in your life is one of the most wonderful, rewarding experiences you'll ever have, and if you do it right it can be a relationship that stays in your heart forever.

To keep the behaviour of your dog submissive, do as Caesar Milan says – remain calm and dominant and keep your dog calm and submissive. They will be happier and so will any other dogs and people be that come into contact with you and your dog.

1. Crating

There is a bit of controversy and well-argued ideas about crating dogs. The correct use of crates is as a place of safety for the dog. It can be used to shut the dog in for a couple of hours at the most. This is useful if the dog frets around certain people, to keep them safe from visiting children and to calm them down when they are over excited. The crate should be a place of safety that the dog is never "forced" into; don't push or shove them into their crate, as this will create a negative association with the crate in the dog's mind. You can entice the dog into the crate with treats. It should have a nice, comfy bed, a water bowl and something to chew on. There should also be a puppy pad if your dog isn't house trained yet, so that any pee doesn't leak onto bedding, which is a horrible thing to let happen. Crating is NOT for your convenience. It is NOT for punishment. It is NOT for long-term use. It is NOT for house training – whatever you read on forums, crating doesn't help with this. It is NOT for your dog to live in. Your dog is a member of the family, not a caged bird.

Against crating

The arguments against crating are many and varied. PETA say that crating is very cruel because it "deprives dogs of the opportunity to fulfil some of their most basic needs, such as the freedom to walk around, the opportunity to relieve themselves and the ability to stretch out and relax. It also prevents them from interacting with their environment and learning how to behave in a human setting."

Crating doesn't help with house training and it is cruel to expect them to hold their bladder or sit in a pool of their own pee. Until your puppy is about 6 months old (with some it can take longer) they won't have enough bladder control to stop themselves from having accidents in the house. Keep them in the kitchen overnight with puppy pads or newspapers in one corner – see housetraining section of this book.

Being in a crate for an extended period of time can cause all sorts of stress and psychological problems. If you crate a dog for any length of time you can cause aggression, hyperactivity, muscle loss, poor bonding, withdrawal and depression. Dogs who are territorial over the house can be made more so if their crate is their territory, and they can get very aggressive if you encroach on their crate territory.

For crating

Properly used dog crates can be a place of safety and calm. Dogs who have been properly crated will go to their crate to sleep out of their own choice. Nervous dogs can gain confidence much more quickly if they know that they can go and be safe whenever they want. My neighbour has a rescue Pomeranian who was badly abused, and really struggled to settle. Eventually they got a crate for her. She was never put in it, but she had her things in there, and blankets and treats and water. Whenever she feels nervous, or there are new people in the house, she can go and hide away until she feels safe to come out. Now she doesn't spend the whole day cowering under things and will happily approach new people in her own time.

Training your dog isn't just to make your life easier, it teaches the dog what the boundaries are and makes them feel more secure. Having a dog in your life can be one of the most rewarding experiences, but it can also be a nightmare. Not knowing how to train a dog can be quite daunting, but with the correct methods and systems in place, training your dog can be something the whole family can be involved in. The real key, however, is to avoid these dogs in the first place. Many people who choose dog ownership go into it with the best intentions but somehow don't quite manage to keep up the training. It is better for you and your dog if the dog is well trained. If an animal knows where it stands and what the boundaries are it will never need to push them.

All dogs want to be part of a pack, and as such, a pet dog will see you as their pack. They need to know exactly where they stand within the pack and that needs to be at the bottom. Harsh as this may seem, if the dog doesn't know that it is below all of the people it may try to assert it's dominance over anyone below it, including children. When a dog tries to become dominant, you can have a very dangerous situation on your hands.

Remember:

- Make sure your dog knows who is in charge.

- Only reward positive behaviour with attention and where safe ignore unwanted behaviours.

- Keep your dog exercised.

- Don't let them get bored.

- Make time for them whenever you can.

There are important things to be aware of when planning for your dog that you might not have considered. These things need to be decided on and agreed by everyone involved in looking after or spending time with the dog. Consensus is important for consistency and it is consistency that will give your dog a good, strong basis on which to start your training.

Choose a name for your dog that is practical and sensible. You might like the name "Princess Conswala of Burm" but it is not a useful name to be calling on a dark night in a park. Also, it would be quite difficult for the dog to recognise. A dog's name needs to be relatively short and should end in a definite vowel sound. This helps a dog to recognise its name and can be useful if there are other dogs around. The vowel sound is what makes our voice unique.

2. Teaching basic first commands

It is important to use distinct sounds and that they are recognisable in your voice, and instructions should be short words with easily identifiable sounds so that your dog can understand what is expected of it. For example, if you teach your dog to stop using the word "wait" and to pee or poop on command using the word "make" you could end up with some unusual and embarrassing mistakes being made.

When teaching your new dog to sit, I usually tend to use "sit" where the main sound is the 'it' at the end, concentrating on the hard 't'. I use the hand signal of an upward facing flat palm and bring my hand up towards my face.

For teaching the dog to wait, whether before it eats its food, at roads or when it's wandered off too far on a walk, I use "stop" where the main sound is the 'op' at the end of the word. The hand signal I use for this is a hand facing outwards like a traffic warden.

Stay is a different command, as I will be walking away from the dog and not towards it, here I use "stay" where the main sound is 'ay'. I use the same hand signal for this as I use for stop.

To call the dog I will say "come" in a higher pitched, clipped voice, so that is it one quick sound. Hand signals aren't very useful here.

Lying down is not a necessary skill for a dog, but can be useful. I say "lie", as it is quite a short sound. The usual hand signal for this is a flat palm facing down, moving towards the ground in a smooth motion.

To get the dog to let go of something or put it down I say "drop" where the main sound is the 'ro' in the middle of the word. I point at the dog.

To encourage the dog to do its business quickly I'll say "make" where the main sound is the 'may' at the beginning. This isn't one that needs a hand signal.

The person doing most of the initial training needs to be the boss. Like all pack animals, dogs need to know who is in charge of what and who the leader is. This reduces confusion and makes the dog much more amenable to training. It also lays a foundation for a happy pack. The role of pack leader doesn't mean that you should be the biggest or loudest in the house. What it does mean is that you should be in control, both of yourself and of the situation (and treats, obviously), so when training first begins there should only be one person doing the majority of the training. After the dog has the hang of the basics, other people can join in. This will cement the positions of where everyone is in the family, and avoid problems of dominance. Everyone must be consistent, though, about what instructions and hand signals you use, about what warrants a treat and about how much of the treat to give them. If there are children helping to train, make sure they know what type of voice to use and not to scream and shout at the dog for getting it wrong. – the dog will either see this as playful and jump about or take it as a threat and become frightened of the child.

When most of people start to think about training a dog, they worry about time. They shouldn't. It isn't very time consuming at all, and can fit in around other commitments. The real time comes in keeping the dog entertained and exercised. You only really need to train a dog for 10 to 15 minuets a day. This may seem like a very short time, but learning new things is a difficult thought process and the brain is the most energy expensive organ in the body. Tired or resentful dogs and puppies don't learn very well at all. Too little time is also not good, as the dog won't retain as much information from shorter training sessions.

You should decide early on what it is that you want to teach your puppy. Make decisions now, you can always add more later, but decide now which bits are absolutely necessary. This will mean that everyone involved knows what is being aimed at. You will need to teach them so sit, to come when called and to stop. Everything else is icing. Stay and lie down can be useful a lot of the time too. Fetching and dropping are usually fairly easy to teach, but if you have other small pets it is important that your dog learns to drop on command, every time – if your dog eats the rabbit it is not the dog's fault, it is yours.

The most important long-term tool in your kit is praise; praise is a fantastic reward for dogs once they have learned to crave your approval. They learn this very early on. As pack animals they want to be loved and appreciated for what they are doing and a great way to show this is by praise.

Treats are usually going to be the basic bribe you are going to use to train your dog. Decide early on what you are going to use as treats and only use them to reward wanted behaviours, and at the beginning of the training time, so that they know what they are working for. With Cavachons there is no real concern about weight problems, so most dog treats will be suitable.

You're ready to start training your dog. Speak in a consistent, midrange tone until you are using the command. Let them know that you have the treat.

Tone of voice is very important for a dog. You need a relatively low, consistent voice and this reflects that you are calm and in control. A high-pitched voice can be seen as a sign of excitement. You can use a higher pitch to praise your dog.

Teaching your dog to come is probably the first thing you should want to teach your dog. Start in a small space where you are confident that the dog won't run off. You might want to do this in a room of your house. When they come towards you, say "come!" in a slightly higher register, and their name, and when they get to you, give them the treat. Then when they wander off again, call them. If they make the connection quickly, they will come to you very quickly. Each time the dog comes to you, say "come" again and give the treat and a big fuss. Once the dog has got the hang of this, get someone to hold them not too far away. Then, when the dog is released, call them until they come to you, and give them the treat. Then try it from further and further away, giving lots of praise and strokes and fuss as well as the treat each time they do it right. This should come quite quickly to most dogs, but with some it may need a bit of persistence.

a) Sit

Teaching your dog to sit is relatively easy, especially if you have a particularly food-centred dog. Let the dog know that you have the treat. Let them know it's in your hand. Stand upright in font of the dog. Put the treat on your hand, palm up and move it above their head. The dog should automatically sit. When they do, say "sit" and give them the treat and a fuss. If they walk backwards instead of sitting, you could get someone to stand behind the dog. Repeating this whenever possible, without tiring out the dog, will mean they learn this very quickly. If the dog seems to be struggling with this, you can put a little light pressure on the back as you give the command. Do not push the dog's back down; this could not only hurt the dog, but break the trust. Training is about trust.

b) Stop or wait

Stop or wait is a very important command to teach your dog. It could be a life saving lesson. When properly taught to wait when told, your dog won't run into the road, or frighten nervous people. For this you need a long leash or one of those extendable ones. While walking along with your dog on the lead at a quite short leash, stop walking, and tell the dog to "stop". When the dog stops pulling you can move on. The dog will soon learn that the sooner he stops pulling, the sooner he will get his way and be able to walk on. This will help you to teach the dog that you are in charge. You are in charge in that the dog will be happier if it just does as you are instructing it.

c) Stay

Once your Cavachon puppy can reliably "Sit", say the word "Stay" and hold your outstretched arm, palm open toward their head and back away a few steps.

If they try to follow, calmly say "No" and put them back into "Sit". Give a treat and then say again, "Stay" with the hand signal and back away a few steps.

Once your puppy is sitting and staying, you can then ask them to "Come". Don't forget to use the open arms hand signal for "Come." Be a little excited with the "Come" command so that your puppy will always enjoy correctly responding and immediately returning to you.

Practice these three basic commands everywhere you go, and use the "Sit" command every time you go for a walk, before you open the door, after you are on the other side of the door, before you go down the stairs, once you are at the bottom of the stairs, and every time you stop when you are on your walk, and pretty soon you will have a puppy who automatically sits whenever you stop moving.

As your puppy gets older, and their attention span increases, you will be able to train for longer periods of time.

d) Lie down

Lie down, while not necessary, can be a really useful command to be able to give under some circumstances. With this method, you need to have already taught "sit". Get the dog to sit, but do not give the treat – keep it in your hand. Then point to or tap on the floor below the dogs nose as they are sitting. The dog should lie down. If they don't, you can apply a small amount of pressure on the shoulders, but not much. If you hurt your dog it will resent training and probably you. As I've already said, training is about trust. Once the dog lies down, say "lie down" and give the treat. Then, after doing this for a while, you can try saying the command and pointing before the dog lies down. Once they've got the hang of this, stand up and do the whole thing from standing until the dog has learned the trick.

e) Drop

Teaching your dog to drop may seem like a daunting task, but it can be relatively easy. When the dog is chewing something they shouldn't be, or even something they should be, you should see this as an opportunity to teach drop. Get your treat ready and stand near the dog. Say "drop" in a low, firm voice, and show them the treat. The dog should open her mouth and pant in anticipation of food. When the item is dropped pick it up and give the treat. Then you can either give back whatever was being chewed or carried or take it away.

f) Come

While most puppies are capable of learning commands and tricks, the first and most important command you need to teach your puppy is the recall, or *"Come"* command.

The hand signal for "Come" is your arms spread wide open. This is a command they can see from a great distance.

Begin the "Come" command inside your home. Go into a larger room, such as your living room area. Place your puppy in front of you and attach their leash or a longer line to their collar while you back away from them a few feet.

Say the command "Come" in an excited voice and hold your arms open wide. If they do not immediately come to you, gently give a tug on the leash so that they understand that they are supposed to move towards you. When they come to you praise them and give a treat they really enjoy.

Once your puppy can accomplish a "Come" command almost every time inside your home, you can then graduate them to a nearby park or quiet outside area where you will repeat the process.

You may want to purchase an extra long line (25 or 50 feet) so that you are always attached to your Cavachon puppy and can encourage them in the right direction should they become distracted.

3. Hand signals

Hand signal training is by far the most useful and efficient training method for every dog, including the Cavachon.

This is because all too often we inundate our canine companions with a great deal of chatter and noise that they really do not understand because English is not their first language.

Contrary to what some humans might think, the first language of a Cavachon, or any dog, is a combination of sensing energy and watching body language, which requires no spoken word or sound.

Therefore, when we humans take the time to teach our dog hand signals for all their basic commands, we are communicating with them at a level they instinctively understand, plus we are helping them to become great followers, as they must watch us to understand what is required of them.

a) Come

When first teaching hand signals to your Cavachon, always show the hand signal for the command at the same time you say the word. If they are totally ignoring the command, it will be time to incorporate a lunge line, which is a very long leash to help you teach the "Come" command.

☑ **Come**: you can kneel down for this command or stay standing. Open your arms wide like you are hugging a very large tree. This hand signal can be seen from a long distance.

Simply attach a 20-foot line to their collar and let them sniff about in a large yard or at your local park.

At your leisure, firmly ask them to "Come" and show the hand signal. If they do not immediately come to you, give a firm tug with the lunge line, so that they understand what you are asking of them.

If they still do not "Come" towards you, simply reel them in until they are in front of you. Then let them wander about again, until you are ready to ask them to "Come".

Repeat this process until your Cavachon responds correctly at least 80% of the time. You can also reinforce the command by giving a treat when they come back to you when asked. Always ask them to "Sit" when they return to you.

b) Sit

☑ **Sit**: right arm (palm open facing upward) parallel to the floor, and then raise your arm, while bent at the elbow toward your shoulder.

Sit is a very simple, yet extremely valuable command for all puppies and dogs.

If your dog is not sitting on command, try holding a treat above and slightly behind their head, so that when they look up for it they may automatically sit to see it.

Slowly remove the treats as reward and replace the treat with a "life reward", such as a chest rub or thumbs up signal and your smile.

If your Cavachon is not particularly treat motivated, lift up and slightly back on the leash when asking them to sit (stand in front of them), and if they still are having difficulties, reach down with your free hand, place it across your dog's back at the place where the back legs join the hip and gently squeeze.

Do NOT simply push down on your dog's back to force their hind legs to collapse under them as this pressure could harm their spine or leg joints.

c) Stay

☑ **Stay**: right arm fully extended toward your dog's head, palm open, hand bent up at the wrist.

Once your Cavachon is in the "Sit" position, ask them to "Stay" with both the verbal cue and the hand signal.

TIP: if you are right-handed, use your right arm and hand for the signal, and if you are left-handed, use your left arm and hand for the signal. Using your dominant hand will be much more effective because your strongest energy emanates from the palm of your dominant hand.

While your dog is sitting and staying, slowly back away from them. If they move from their position, calmly put them back into sit and ask them to "Stay" again, using both the verbal cue and the hand signal.

Continue to practice this until your dog understands that you want them to stay sitting and not move towards you.

With all commands, when your Cavachon is just learning, be patient and always reward them with a treat and your happy praise for a job well done.

4. Simple tricks

When teaching your Cavachon tricks, in order to give them extra incentive, find a treat that they really like, and give the treat as rewards and to help solidify a good performance. Most dogs will be extra attentive during training sessions when they know that they will be rewarded with their favourite treats.

If your Cavachon is less than six months old when you begin teaching them tricks, keep your training sessions short (no more than 5 or 10 minutes) and fun, and as they become adults you can extend your sessions as they will be able to maintain their focus for longer periods of time.

a) Shake a Paw

Who doesn't love a dog that knows how to shake a paw? This is one of the easiest tricks to teach your Cavachon.

TIP: most dogs are naturally either right or left pawed. If you know which paw your dog favours, ask them to shake this paw.

Find a quiet place to practice, without noisy distractions or other pets, and stand or sit in front of your dog. Place them in the sitting position and have a treat in your left hand.

Say the command *"Shake"* while putting your right hand behind their left or right paw and pulling the paw gently toward yourself until you are holding their paw in your hand. Immediately praise them and give them the treat.

Most dogs will learn the "Shake" trick very quickly, and very soon, once you put out your hand, your Cavachon will immediately lift their paw and put it into your hand, without your assistance or any verbal cue.

Practice every day until they are 100% reliable with this trick, and then it will be time to add another trick to their repertoire.

b) Roll Over

You will find that just like your Cavachon is naturally either right or left pawed, that they will also naturally want to roll either to the right or the left side. Take advantage of this by asking your dog to roll to the side they naturally prefer.

Sit with your dog on the floor and put them in a lie down position. Hold a treat in your hand and place it close to their nose without allowing them to grab it, and while they are in the lying position, move the treat to the right or left side of their head so that they have to roll over to get to it.

You will very quickly see which side they want to naturally roll to, and once you see this, move the treat to this side. Once they roll over to this side, immediately give them the treat and praise them.

You can say the verbal cue *"Over"* while you demonstrate the hand signal motion (moving your right hand in a circular motion) or moving the treat from one side of their head to the other with a half circle motion.

Once your Cavachon can roll over every time you ask, it will be time to teach them another trick.

c) Sit Pretty

While this trick is a little more complicated, and most dogs pick up on it very quickly. Remember that every dog is different so always exercise patience.

Find a quiet space with few distractions and sit or stand in front of your dog and ask them to "Sit".

Have a treat nearby (on a countertop or table) and when they sit, use both of your hands to lift up their front paws into the sitting pretty position, while saying the command *"Sit Pretty"*. Help them balance in this position while you praise them and give them the treat.

Once your Cavachon can do the balancing part of the trick quite easily without your help, sit or stand in front of your dog while asking them to *"Sit Pretty"* and hold the treat above their head, at the level their nose would be when they sit pretty.

If they attempt to stand on their back legs to get the treat, you may be holding the treat too high, which will encourage them to stand on their back legs to reach it. Go back to the first step and put them back into the *"Sit"* position and again lift their paws while their backside remains on the floor.

The hand signal for *"Sit Pretty"* is a straight arm held over your dog's head with a closed fist.

Make this a fun and entertaining time for your Cavachon and practice a few times every day until they can *"Sit Pretty"* on hand signal command every time you ask.

A young Cavachon puppy should be able to easily learn these basic tricks before they are six months old and when you are patient and make your training sessions short and fun for your dog, they will be eager to learn more.

5. Adult Training

When your Cavachon is a fully grown adult (approximately two years of age), now is the time that you can begin more complicated or advanced training sessions. They will enjoy it and when you have the desire and patience, there is no end to the tricks you can teach a willing Cavachon.

For instance, you may wish to teach your adult Cavachon more advanced tricks, such as how to dance, or the opposite paw shake or side roll over, which are more difficult than you might expect.

If you and your Cavachon are really enjoying learning new tricks together, you might want to advance to teaching them the *"commando crawl"*, how to *"speak"* or to *"jump through the human hoop"*. All of these tricks are fun to teach and will exercise both your Cavachon's body and mind.

As well, the more control you have over your Cavachon, the easier it will be to teach them a fun sport, such as Agility.

The only restriction to how far you can go with training your adult Cavachon will be your imagination and their personal ability or desire to perform.

6. Good habits

You don't want to get into a situation where you have to undo unwanted behaviours, so the best thing to do is to lay down strong foundations. There are a few things you can do to encourage only good behaviours and leave no room for bad ones.

The most important thing you can do for your dog – and you might get bored of me saying this, but it's very important – is to establish yourself as the pack leader. This doesn't mean be aggressive or hurting your dog, it means making your dog feel secure and safe in the knowledge that all they have to do is be a good dog. The way you establish this at an early stage is by not putting up with any nonsense. This includes climbing up on you uninvited, pushing a toy into you or pawing in order to get you to play with them or nudging you to get attention, becoming annoyed if they get disturbed while sleeping, resting or eating. If your dog likes to sleep on top of humans, that's also a sign of dominance. Your dog shouldn't lick you if don't want them to. They shouldn't lick you to get attention or while you're doing something else. If your dog starts carrying himself or herself with a proud gait, head held high then you need to discourage this. The head shouldn't be too high and the tail shouldn't be held much higher above the body. The dog shouldn't be allowed to sit in high places, looking down on everything. If they refuse to walk on a lead when they are healthy adults, this is another sign of dominance and shouldn't be stood for. Nipping at people's heels when they are leaving should always be corrected – this is your dog saying "I didn't say you could go". This behaviour will also soon stop your friends and family from visiting you too. If at any point your dog stops listening to known commands, you know that they are not listening to you. They are showing dominance. If you find your dog guarding you or your family from others approaching, some people like to call it "protecting" but it's actually "claiming" that dog owns you. Persistence about being on a particular piece of furniture when asked to stay off is a sign that the dog thinks he or she owns it. If the dog sounds like they're screaming or in distress when they don't want to do something but you find there is no way they're in pain this is a control mechanism. Correct the behaviour immediately.

By giving your dog enough exercise and entertainment can mean that you never have to deal with any behavioural problems.

By praising even the most mundane activities, such as sitting without being asked (not at the dinner table, this is begging and should not be encouraged), lying on the floor or in their bed, eating from their bowl and running about outside, you can give your dog positive ways to get your attention.

The first time your dog jumps up you should stop this becoming an attention seeking habit. Without making eye contact or speaking to the dog, take its paws, and replace them on the ground, gently. If they jump up again, repeat this until they wait on the ground. You might want to tell them to sit. Then, when they are calmly on the ground, give them a big fuss. Being on the ground nicely and calmly is wanted behaviour, so reward this with praise.

Hyperactivity can be caused by all manner of things, but often it is pent up energy, uncertainty and a reaction to its surroundings. (If hyperactivity is combined with weight loss and an increased appetite, consult your vet.) Dogs are pack animals and they get a lot of their behaviours from where they fit into the pack. They also look to you. They feed off of your energy and react to the rest of the pack- if you are doing things that confuse or upset the dog, if you send mixed messages or if you behave in a way the dog considers hyperactive, the dog will be come hyperactive.

Because of this you should try to keep an eye on your own energy and be very aware of how you are around your dog. You need to be calm and assertive. You need to be the pack leader and the pack leader always knows what's going on and is calm. If you're worried about something at work or stressed about an argument, your dog will pick up on the anxiety and translate it to himself or herself. I find that if I'm stressed by something, it helps to stretch my shoulders and straighten my back as far as it will comfortably go, before I attempt to interact with dogs.

By simply ignoring the hyperactive behaviour, you can begin to put it right.

Your dog wants your attention. By paying any attention to unwanted behaviour you are rewarding it. If the behaviour isn't dangerous you should ignore it. The next time the dog is bouncing about like a lunatic or yapping away, simply ignore it. Don't look at them, don't touch them, and don't talk to them. It's amazing how fast the dog will calm down.

Use up the excess energy.

If your dog has too much built-up energy, take them for a long walk. Play 20 minutes of fetch. Once you've burned that extra energy away, your dog should be nice and relaxed and sleepy. Some owners that are at work a lot use a fetch machine, which the dog can load itself when it wants something to do. Exercise has a calming effect on dogs, not just people, and a good run can do a dog the world of good.

Most dog breads were originally working dogs. They need something to do.

Having something to do on can help so much. Hyperactivity in your dog can be a sign of psychological needs as much as it can of physical needs. By giving your dog a job to do, you are taking the hyper energy and putting it into something constructive. For

122

instance, having your dog carry something around with it in its mouth or in one of those doggy backpacks with extra weight will keep your dog focused on carrying instead of getting distracted by squirrels and other things.

If all else fails, have a go at aromatherapy.

A dog's world is coloured by scent. Lots of interesting smells around the home and garden can distract dogs, making them feel frustrated and uneasy. In the same way, there are lots of scents that can calm a dog. I recommend to the owners I work with that they grow lavender. A dog rubbed with lavender flowers will just bliss out very quickly and have a little nap. There are all sorts of lavender diffusers around if you don't want to grow it, from the little plug in things to fancy whirly things that light up. Nice as the candle and oil burners are, naked flames aren't particularly safe, especially if your dog wants to get a good whiff of them. Candles + dog = fire.

7. Bad habits

Many of us humans make the mistake of allowing a crying puppy to sleep with them in their bed, and while this may help to calm and comfort a new puppy, it will set a dangerous precedent that can result in behavioural problems later on in his/her life.
Don't let them sleep in your bed – you can get all sorts of diseases from sleeping dogs and letting them sleep in your bed with you can set them up for bad, possessive and dominant behaviours later in life. Not only this, but a tiny Cavachon puppy can easily be crushed by a sleeping human body.
As much as it may pull on your heart strings to hear your new Cavachon puppy crying the first couple of nights in their kennel, a little tough love at the beginning will help them to learn to both love and respect you as their leader.
Never pick your puppy up if they display fear or growl at an object or person, because this will be rewarding them for unbalanced behaviour.

Instead, your puppy needs to be gently corrected by you, with firm and calm energy so that they learn not to react with fear or aggression.

Many humans play too hard or allow their children to play too long with a young puppy. You need to remember that a young puppy tires very easily and especially during the critical growing phases of their young life, they need their rest.

Always discourage your Cavachon puppy from chewing or biting your hands, or any part of your body for that matter. If you allow them to do this when they are puppies, they will want to continue to do so when they have strong jaws and adult teeth and this is not acceptable behaviour for any breed of dog.

Do not get into the habit of playing the *"hand"* game, where you rough up the puppy and slide them across the floor with your hands, because this will teach your puppy that your hands are playthings.

Destructive behaviour and chewing can be a real pain. It can be frustrating and upsetting for you as an owner and bad for your dog's health.

The first thing you need to do is make sure there are no medical problems.

Nutritional deficiencies caused by poor diet early on in their life or now, and/or some sort of parasite can lead to something called "pica". Pica is a condition in people and animals where they have an urge to eat non-nutritive (not food) things. This is something that needs to be treated differently, which may be misconstrued as inappropriate chewing. Gastrointestinal problems may cause an unsettled stomach, which can make the dog start chewing to help cope with the nausea.

8. Transfer chewing to something more appropriate

Give your dog chew toys that are safe and that they are allowed. Chewing is a natural behaviour. Be careful with rawhide and beef bones as some dogs can chew them into very small bits that can be choked on. Avoid chicken bones too, as small bits of splintered bone can do all manner of damage and chicken bones splinter very easily. I usually tend to use pigs ears and dental chews, since they encourage appropriate chewing while combating dental disease. Rubber chew balls are also brilliant, as they allow a dog to get to their chew on. You need to get something of the right size. They should be able to pick it up and carry it but it should be of sufficient bulk that it cannot be swallowed.

The dog shouldn't be able to do much damage now, but if they're still chewing inappropriately, speak in a very low voice, almost a rumbling growl. Then direct their attention to something they're allowed to chew on and praise the correct behaviour.

Biting can be a very worrying problem. You love your dog but they have begun to bite and you know how dangerous this can be. This isn't the end of the world if you nip it in the bud (no pun intended). A few simple rules will keep you out of such a situation, but if you are very worried about biting, never be afraid to call on professional help.

9. Don't start rough games

Once you get involved in play fights, or even fast paced/energetic games of fetch, you could get accidentally bitten. This isn't always the dog's intention - they grip with their mouth. If you're wrestling, this could mean your arm or leg. Once the dog has learned to "drop" then you shouldn't need to physically take a ball out of the dog's mouth.

10. Make your dog submissive

Your dog should know that they are bottom of the pack. If they are comfortable and secure with their position in the pack, they won't vie for a higher position.

11. Get your dog 'done'

If you get your dog spayed or neutered, this will radically reduce any aggression they might exhibit. It is also good for population control and reduces the likelihood of hormone and reproductive related cancers. As well as this, your dog is less likely to be injured by other dogs. While it can sometimes be difficult to find the authoritative answer about when is the best time to neuter or spay your young Cavachon, because there are varying opinions on this topic, one thing that most veterinarians will agree on is that earlier spaying or neutering is best. Female dogs can be spayed from about 6 months onwards, and most vets will want to wait until male dogs are 7 months old.

Spaying or neutering surgeries are carried out under general anaesthesia, which does carry risks, but is safer in the long run than leaving your dog unprotected.

More dogs are being neutered at younger ages, so speak with your veterinarian and ask for their recommendations regarding the right age to spay or neuter your Cavachon.

While neutering or spaying is not a treatment for aggression, it can certainly help to minimize the severity and escalation of aggressiveness and is often the first step towards resolving an aggressive behaviour problem.

Neutering is a surgical procedure carried out by a licensed veterinarian surgeon, which renders a male dog unable to reproduce.

In males, the surgery is also referred to as *"castration"* because the procedure entails the removal of the young dog's testicles. When the testicles are removed, what is left behind is an empty scrotal sac (which used to contain the puppy's testicles) and this empty sac will soon shrink in size until it is no longer noticeable. Neutering can also mean that a male dog will be less likely to have the urge to wander.

Non-neutered males also tend to spray or mark territory far more often both inside and outside the home, and during this time can start to display aggressive tendencies toward other dogs as well as people

In female puppies, sterilization, referred to as *"spaying"* is a surgical procedure carried out by a licensed veterinarian to

126

prevent the female dog from becoming pregnant and to stop regular heat cycles.

The sterilization procedure is much more involved for a female puppy (than for a male), as it requires the removal of both ovaries and the uterus by incision into the puppy's abdominal cavity. The uterus is also removed during this surgery to prevent the possibility of it becoming infected later on in life.

Preferably, female Cavachon puppies should be spayed before their very first oestrus or heat cycle. Females in heat often appear more agitated and irritable while sleeping and eating less and some may become extremely aggressive towards other dogs.

Spaying female puppies before their first heat pattern can eliminate these hormonal stressors and reduce the opportunity of mammary glandular tumours. Early spaying also protects against various other potential concerns, such as uterine infections.

Many dog owners often become needlessly worried that a neutered or spayed dog will lose their vigour. Rest assured that a dog's personality or energy level will not be modified by neutering, and in fact, many unfavourable qualities resulting from hormonal impact may resolve after surgery.

Your Cavachon will certainly not come to be less caring or cheerful, and neither will it resent you because you are not denying your dog any essential encounters. You will, however, be acting as an accountable, informed, and caring Cavachon owner. Furthermore, there is little evidence to suggest that the nature of a female Cavachon will improve after having a litter of puppies.

It is important that you do not place your own psychological needs or concerns onto your Cavachon puppy, because there is no gain to be had from permitting sexual activity in either male or female canines.

It is not *"abnormal"* or *"mean"* to manage a puppy's reproductive activity by having them sterilized. Rather, it is unkind not to neuter or spay a dog and there are many benefits of having this procedure carried out.

A neutered or spayed Cavachon is less likely to wander. Castrated male dogs have the tendency to patrol smaller sized, outdoor areas and are less likely to participate in territorial conflicts with perceived opponents.

A Cavachon that has actually already had successful escapes from the yard may continue to wander after they are spayed or neutered.

An unsterilized dog may urinate or defecate inside the home or in other undesirable areas in an attempt to stake territorial claims, relieve anxiety, or to advertise their available reproductive status.

While neutering or spaying a Cavachon puppy after they have already begun to inappropriately eliminate or mark territory to announce their sexual availability to other dogs will reduce the more powerful urine odour as well as eliminate the hormonal factors, once this habit has begun, the undesirable behaviour may continue to persist after neutering or spaying.

While metabolic changes that occur after spaying or neutering can cause some Cavachon puppies to gain weight, often the real culprit for any weight gain is the human who feels guilty for subjecting their puppy to any kind of pain and therefore they attempt to make themselves feel better by feeding more treats or meals to their Cavachon companion.

If you are concerned about weight gain after neutering or spaying a Cavachon puppy, simply adjust their food and treat consumption as needed.

It is a very simply process to change your Cavachon's food intake according to their physical demands and how they look, and if your Cavachon puppy's daily exercise and level of activity has not changed after they have been spayed or neutered, there will likely be no change in food management necessary.

12. Don't leave any dog alone with little ones

It goes without saying, don't do it. It's not a good idea. There's no situation where you should leave a dog with a baby or child. Even if the dog dotes on the children, they could accidentally damage the children, either with rough play or misplaced affection. Dogs carry their young in their mouths. If a dog picks up or tries to move a child using their mouth they could do so much damage. It's not worth it.

13. Show who's in charge

It is important that you practice activities that encourage calm submission. Dogs need to know their position at the bottom of the pack. So encourage a calm-submissive state before engaging in any activity. Once your dog understands that they must be calm and controlled around the house and before they get to play, they will not be so interested and obsessed with the things around them.

14. Distraction

You also need to condition your dog's brain to react differently to their tail or shadows or the child/person. When you're walking the dog or playing in the garden, don't let them see the object of their obsession. Keep him/her focused on the task in hand. Make this her mental challenge. You could try putting a dog backpack on your dog with water bottles for added weight to get him/her focused on carrying things.

One thing a lot of dog owners think is bad behaviour or bad for their dog is grass eating. This is really not something you should worry about as long as the grass has not been treated with any chemicals – in public places where grass has been treated with pesticides it is usually sign posted, but the safest grass is in your garden – you know exactly what's on it. If the dog is vomiting because of eating grass, then it should be discouraged. Dogs are not naturally carnivores, their diet should include some vegetation and eating grass may well be a natural instinct. Also, grass provides roughage and does a similar job in dogs as bran does in humans; it's good for their digestion. If the grass eating becomes a compulsive behaviour it needs to be discouraged by distracting them.

Do not hit your dog. This may seem obvious, but a beaten dog will not trust you. There are far more effective 'punishments'. I use a variety of methods to discourage unwanted behaviours at an early stage. All physical contact with their human should be positive, and will be seen as a reward for being good. All contact with their owner should be treasured by the dog, as a reward for not being bad.

The tone of your voice is an amazingly strong tool in dog training. Cavachons respond even better to tone of voice than a lot of other breeds, as they are bred from working dogs. Like very young children, they can't understand the words, but they can understand tone of voice. A calm, level register is very good for the dog. Talk to them in a soothing, deep voice and they will be calm. If they are doing something that you want them to stop doing right now, "NO!" isn't always enough. It has to be said in a low rumble, almost like a growl. This is an unambiguous command. The tone of your voice registers as disapproval. If you say it in a high tone, the dog will see this as a sign that you are excited by what they are doing - they can't understand the words. A high-pitched tone is, in fact, a fantastic reward. "Good dog!" only woks if you sound like you mean it. Even if you're feeling overheated or tired and apathetic, fake it. Your dog will appreciate the sound and won't recognize the insincerity.

A simple touch can be so rewarding. Whether you're working with bad dogs or grumpy teenagers, a strong, encouraging hand on the shoulder can work wonders. If the dog is feeling a little down – and they do get down – a firm but gentle touch can be all it takes to make them feel better. It can also have a wonderful calming affect on an over active or stressed dog. Just calmly leave your hand on their shoulder for a few seconds.

By petting your dog to placate or appease them, you are giving positive attention. The dog is getting what they want from you by doing this behaviour. They will learn very quickly that this behaviour gets them petted and they will do it as an attention seeking measure. It is very hard not to fuss your dog if they are bouncing about and being excited at you but this is how people get accidentally bitten. Pet your dog when they are being good.

This could even be when they are just lounging about the house or lying on the grass.

Eye contact is an important communication of trust. Dogs often see this as condoning their behaviour. You are looking at them like you love them. So avoid eye contact. I have even, with some very persistent attention seekers, physically blocked eye contact by putting my hand between my eyes and the dogs, without touching the dog. The dog with then make an effort to seem calm.

Attention, even negative attention, can be seen as a reward. The dog wants your attention and withholding it can work tremendously well. Be very careful not to inadvertently reward unwanted behaviours. A very effective way to discipline your dog is to ignore them. This might feel horrid, but it is one of the best 'punishments' you can use.

Treats should be healthy and used sparingly. Most commercially available dog treats are relatively healthy for your dog. In summer, you might want to freeze some dog food in an ice cube tray to use as rewards. Carrots are very good for your dog, are often very well received and also help keep the teeth clean.

15. Behavioural problems

The number of Cavachons and other 'designer' dogs coming into rescue centres is at an all time high. Many of them have behavioural problems because of lack of training or even because of human abuse. The upsetting thing is that you can find Cavachons in dog shelters across the UK and USA. Re-homing an abandoned dog can be the most rewarding experience. If you choose a rescue dog, you need to be aware of where they came from. A lot of rescued Cavachons are relatively well behaved and you can continue training them as you would any other puppy or dog. Some of them, however, may need a lot of work. You could find yourself with a traumatised or aggressive dog.

This may seem like a horrific situation to find yourself in, but it is far more common than you'd think. While these dogs take a lot more time and energy, many of them can be saved by correct training, a lot of time and trust building. Many people who chose dog ownership go into it with the best intentions but somehow don't quite manage to keep up the training, or circumstances change and for whatever reason they end up with a badly trained, badly behaved dog. Often, this can be rectified with a few simple techniques.

16. Retraining

So you've already got a bad dog. What do you do next? The key thing with animals that haven't had completely positive histories with humans is trust. Nervous dogs are not just nervous of you- don't take it personally. Regaining trust can be a long and difficult process, but if you think you have the patience and the time then the process can be very rewarding.

Building trust in an abused or poorly socialized animal can be a slow, laborious process, but it can also be incredibly rewarding. If this process seems to be taking forever, please, please remember that the dog is doing their best. They may have very unpleasant memories of people and if you become frustrated or inconsistent they can become frightened.

Proximity and trust

For this you will need a room where you can sit with the dog, but not trying to touch or even talk to it. Get comfy with a book. You might want to try one of those lavender plug in things, or even lavender plants if you don't mind them getting a bit nibbled. As dogs are very into smell, the calming scent of lavender can really work to take the edge off of the tension. A very nervous dog needs somewhere to hide. This may seem counter intuitive, but if you provide hiding places, (not permanently as this causes more issues) then the animal will feel more confident that it can get away when it needs to. You may need to sit in a room with the dog for hours, not engaging at all.

It is also very important that your dog knows where you are when you are in the room. If they can see you, they can defend themselves and will feel more confident.

Leash and collar

With smaller dogs or dogs that are not built to pull, a harness might be a better idea, especially if the dog has had a negative experience with collars. A dog that used to be a 'tied dog' - one that lived its life tied up - can have real problems adjusting to having things around its neck that aren't a source of fear. You want to let the dog get used to the collar and leash or harness for about ten minutes before any walks or outside time. If the dog is especially frightened of this, then you may want to let them have the collar and leash or harness for longer periods without having to be restrained by it on a walk. If you have a well fenced garden you should fit them with the harness or collar and leash and just let them roam about in your garden.

Some very traumatized dogs can become catatonic (unresponsive and still) at having a leach and collar around their neck. These dogs may need to be left with their collar. Just let the collar be in the room with them while they are fed. Then slowly introduce the collar, at feeding times, to the dog, laying the collar on their back, but not fastening it around the neck. Eventually, the dog should accept the collar in connection to food and not trauma.

Physical contact

All physical contact with your dog should be positive anyway. With dogs that have problems trusting people you must be especially careful to remember this. If you are touching your dog it is because they allow it. They are more likely to allow it if you have complete proximity trust and if they are generally rewarded for allowing you to touch them. Remember – positive contact with humans is wanted behaviour. Reward it.

Your behaviour

As the dog's new owner, it is now your responsibility to model consistent, level and above all dependable behaviours. You need to remain calm and constant and to provide a stable home and environment for any animal, but a dog with a bad background needs this more.

Giving your dog enough exercise and entertainment can mean you never have to deal with any behavioural problems.

Undoing unwanted behaviour (stopping them eating the furniture and other bad habits that have already formed) can seem like a real challenge, but a lot of their behaviours are a reflection of the energies they see around them.

Because of this you should try to keep an eye on your own energy and be very aware of how you are around your dog. You need to be calm and assertive. Take a few deep breaths. Cool yourself down. At this exact moment in time you are setting a good example to your dog. You can fume about your boss or neighbour later.

Hyperactivity is often attention seeking nonsense. Make sure they've had enough exercise and entertainment during the day and that they have been walked enough, after that, it's attention seeking. If hyperactivity is combined with weight loss and an increased appetite, consult your vet.

17. Destructive behaviour

Destructive behaviour and chewing can be a real pain. It can be frustrating and upsetting for you as an owner and bad for your dog's health.

The first thing you need to do is make sure there are no medical problems.

Remember, if Pica occurs, you need to treat it.

Dog proof your home

If your dog is a chewer you need to make sure they aren't chewing anything that could make them sick. This means getting anything toxic or poisonous out of their reach. If they're chewing furniture, there are bad tasting sprays you can put on, but some of these can stain so check the labels. There is a great range of things you can spray on.

Transfer chewing to something more appropriate.

If you're stopping the dog chewing your things, give them something that they're allowed to chew. Chewing is a natural behaviour. Avoid chicken bones too, as small bits of splintered bone can do all manner of damage and chicken bones splinter very easily.

If the dog is still doing inappropriate chewing, assert your dominance. You are the leader. "NO" in your deepest voice will stop them while you are there.

Bad dogs that bite can get put down, so you need to make sure this isn't going to happen to your dog. I have put aggression in a separate chapter. Aggressive dogs are bad dogs. But some dogs bite by accident.

Rough and tumble games can end in biting, so you don't want to get involved in these sort of games.

Make sure your dog is spayed or neutered (rescue dogs are almost universally already done).

Make sure your dog knows who is boss.

Don't leave the dog alone with children. Dogs can try to move, protect or dominate children with disastrous consequences. I was bitten by our Tibetan Terrier when I was small. The dog was only 11 inches high. No matter how small or sweet the dog is –don't leave them with the kids.

Obsessive behaviours

Dogs can become obsessed with all kinds of things, tail chasing, shadows or even people. Perhaps they don't recognize their tail as part of them, just as something that keeps on getting away. They may want the shadow, and the fact that they can't have it can be very upsetting. Or more worryingly, they may become obsessed with a member of the family, such as a child that they always want to know where her/she is. If a dog begins to want to herd the children, this is not 'cute'; it is potentially dangerous.

18. Aggression – causes and cures

Dog aggression can be not only a problem that alienates you from your friends and neighbours, but can have serious legal repercussions. Before you can fix the aggression, you need to understand the causes of dog aggression. Once you know why your dog is behaving in this way, you can begin to overcome aggression. Dog aggression stems from the dog's frustration and dominance. The dog's frustration comes from a lack of exercise, and the dog's dominance comes from a lack of calm-assertive leadership.

Is it the breed?

Probably not. Cavachons are generally sweet little things and don't tend to be snappy or aggressive. The cuteness of the breed can lead to them being badly trained though. My brother-in-law's Yorkie is a nightmare because she is pampered and treated all the time. She's always being picked up and fussed over and is never told off because she's "so little, though". He doesn't have many houseguests any more.

Aggression towards dogs

When dogs fight amongst themselves, it is because they can't recognise a main authority. They need to know who the pack leader is. They know who is strong and who will make a good leader. If no one shows leadership then the dogs will challenge each other for it. As soon as your dogs see you as being in charge-

136

you have to be the boss for their peace of mind- the dog on dog aggression will stop.

Dangerous or aggressive dogs

What has to be understood here is that these dogs are frustrated and confused. If you have an aggressive or frightened dog you need to be in control, to be powerful, to be Alfa. You must gain control of the situation and dog behaviour before it escalates. It is a tragedy when a dog has to be destroyed because of its behaviour, and it is usually an avoidable one.

When dealing with these dogs, you need to be the boss. You have to be in charge. You NEED to be pack leader for the dog's sake. If a dog doesn't know where it stands, the poor thing becomes very confused, stressed out and, ultimately, dangerous. Even small dogs can be dangerous. This is a vital part of getting your dog back to being your dog again: changing YOUR behaviour. It needs to be a permanent change and it needs to be a positive one.

Fear

A lot of people begin to be frightened of their dog as it becomes aggressive. This is the wrong response. If you are frightened of your dog you need to get over it or get the dog to someone who isn't afraid. It's that simple. A dog that is around people who are afraid of it will learn that aggression is the way to get what it wants.

Exercise

I've worked with aggressive dogs and aggressive teens. Often there is a fairly simple solution. If there is a lot of pent up energy this can lead to frustration and anxiety, which can easily be transferred to aggression. I do the same thing with aggressive boys as I do with aggressive dogs – put a muzzle on if they bite and take them for a run. Getting all that excess energy stress out of them allows their body and their mind to relax a little more. If you make sure your dog is well exercised they are far less likely to exhibit aggressive behaviour. If you're out a lot you might want to get a fetch machine that the dog loads when it wants to play, or some sort of treat device.

Boredom

Bored dogs are far more likely to exhibit aggressive behaviour. If you are out a lot then you need to keep the dog entertained while you are away. Bob a lots and kongs are brilliant, as the dog has to work to get their treat. There is also something called a tug a jug, where the dog has to pull a rope to get treats. These things keep the animal entertained and reduce stress and anxiety.

19. Run Aways

One thing that all dog owners fear is their dog running away. The ideal situation would be your dog not running away at all. But sometimes, despite our best efforts, they do get away from us. As Cavachons are smaller dogs it can be easier for them to get away. Their size also means that they can't survive as well out of the home, they will cool down dramatically over night, they can get into all sorts of dangerous places when they squeeze their bodies into them and they can become a target for larger predator animals.

However, you must remain calm. They'll probably have a full belly, and a rough idea of where home is in case they get into any bother, or for when they decide their adventure is over and it is home time. There is a story of a dog escaping while his owner was ill and going for the normal walk. The owner, when he realised his dog was missing followed the directions of people who had seen him and it turned out he had just wandered off in the exact circuit that he was walked on, and by the time the owner was home, the dog was too!

The main thing to remember is to keep calm and maintain a happy persona, even if you're worried, while you call out for your dog. If they have a micro chip then they'll come back to you if they're found. If not you need to call all of the local shelters and provide them with a good photograph of your Cavachon.

Chapter 9) Health problems

1. Signs your Cavachon is sick

You need to be on the look out for the following things, and anything out of the ordinary – make note and tell your vet.

Vomiting

Diarrhoea

Frequent urination

Blood in the urine

Accidental urination

Trouble urinating

Thicker that usual urine

Stronger smelling urine

2. Unusual illnesses

Alabama rot-type illness

While this section aims to give advice on the most common health problems, remember that you know your Cavachon. If you are ever worried about the health of your little dog, even if you can't quite put your finger on why, then you should seek veterinary advice. If you keep a good record of anything out of the ordinary that happens in your dog's life then this can help to work out the cause of any problems.

Dogs are incredibly robust animals and are quite good at keeping themselves well, and with the right nutritional care from you, illness in your dog should be very rare. There may be instances, however, when your dog does get unwell. In these circumstances, your quick action can be the difference between a quick, easy recovery and a long, drawn out, expensive and exhausting illness. The usual reason for your dog getting ill is that they've eaten something disgusting. Yes, even the beautiful Cavachon, with their fluffy little faces and their sweet natures, will eat things that make your stomach churn. Usually of the faeces or rotting animal variety, things your little pooch finds can be full of things that could make it ill.

3. Common illnesses

Liver disease

The liver is one of the organs that cleans your blood, removing toxins. It also passes nutrients taken from food and passes it into the blood. It also makes clotting factors and amino acids. It is the liver that keeps the blood useful.

Symptoms include:

Loss in appetite

Sudden weight loss

Lack of energy or depression

Jaundice (yellowing of the gums, whitening of the eyes or skin)

Darker urine

Paleness in the gums

Swollen tummy that is firmer than usual

If you suspect liver disease, if you even suspect any problems at all with the liver, you need to contact your vet. SEEK IMMEDIATE VERTERINARY ATTENTION as Liver disease can be fatal.

There are a number of possible causes that will all be treated differently, and it is important that you can give your vet as much information to work out how this happened. At this point it's a really good idea to be keeping a logbook of anything out of the ordinary so you can provide a detailed history.

Causes of liver disease include:

Poison

Viral and bacterial infections

Restricted blood flow to the liver (because of heart disease or other inherited irregularity)

Lipidosis, where too much fat is released into the blood and is mopped up by the liver

For dogs with liver disorders, veterinarians often recommend very specific nutrition. You could have to make some long-term changes to the diet and lifestyle of your dog if they're diagnosed with liver problems, and while your veterinarian will be able to advise you on these, be prepared to have to:

Feed your dog easily digested carbohydrates, high-quality fats and limited amounts of sodium to control ongoing liver damage and improve liver function.

Increase exercise as health improves.

Medicate regularly based on diagnosis.

Tick paralysis

Not really a problem in the northern hemisphere, but common in Australia and New Zealand, tick paralysis is caused when paralysis ticks secrete a toxin that affects the nervous system. Affected dogs show signs of weakness and limpness approximately one week after being first bitten by ticks. Symptoms usual begin with a change in pitch of the dog's usual bark, which will become more and more feeble as the muscles become paralyzed, and weakness in the rear legs that eventually involves all four legs, which is then followed by the dog showing difficulty breathing and swallowing. If the condition is not diagnosed and treated, death can occur.

Treatment involves locating and removing the tick and treatment with tick anti-serum. In the case of tick paralysis the anti-serum is made using dog's blood and is much more effective on dogs than it is on cats.

Regular grooming can help you find any ticks early. As Cavachons have long, curly hair, ticks can go unnoticed by humans for quite a while.

Heart disease

Just like us, dogs can develop heat disease. Smaller dogs like Cavachons are less prone to heart disease than larger breeds, but they can develop it, especially with weight issues. They are not going to get heart disease for smoking related reasons like humans, but they do have other bad habits than can get their heart into trouble, because of their practice of eating 'yucky' things, nibbling on slugs and licking strangers, they can get something called heartworm.

Hyperthyroidism can cause heart problems too.

Another reason for heart problems in dogs is one that is commonly the problem in people too – obesity. The problem with Cavachons is that they are very cute. Cute and overfeed-able. If your dog is overweight they will be far more prone to a whole host of unpleasant heart problems. They can also develop hypertrophic cardio-myopathy, where the muscle of the ventricle of the heart becomes thickened. They can develop fat in the ventricles. They can develop leaky valves because of the extra pressure of pumping blood around a body bigger than it was designed for.

Symptoms include:

Breathing difficulties and shortness of breath

General apathy

Sudden change in weight

Coughing a lot

Swelling in the body

If you notice any of these symptoms you need to go to your vet as soon as you can. The treatment may be as simple as a short course of medication. It may require surgery, however, and in this case you will be glad of your insurance. Or there may be lifestyle changes you need to make, perhaps a change in diet and activity.

Fleas and worms

Even lap dogs can get fleas. It's not because your house is unclean or because you have poor hygiene. If they do get fleas, they can be treated with capstar tablets or spot on.

Gingivitis

Dogs that have been fed a high-carbohydrate diet become more sensitive to plaque bacteria because of the sugary acids. Mingled with saliva and minerals, plaque can harden into tartar, a yellowish crust that irritates the dog's gums. Left untreated, tartar eventually builds up under the gum, separating it from the teeth. Reddened gums, bad breath and difficulty eating are early signs of gingivitis, which usually begins with one tooth but can spread quickly. This bacterium can spread to other organs through the bloodstream and cause kidney damage.

Symptoms include:

Sensitivity around the mouth

Loss of appetite

Worse than usual breath

Redness in the gums

If you think your dog has gingivitis, go and see your vet before it spreads to other organs. Your vet will clean the teeth and tell you about the follow up care. This may involve antibiotics, but will definitely involve a daily brushing for a while and tooth cleaning toys and treats.

You can avoid gingivitis by giving lots of hard, abrasive treats and carrots. Left untreated, gingivitis can lead to badly inflamed gums.

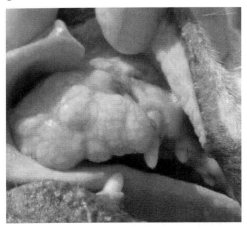

Lymphoma

Lymphoma is the most common cancer in dogs and it originates in white blood cells known as lymphocyte cells. This blood cancer can appear in various parts of your dog's body and affects its immune system. Cancer is everyone's worst nightmare, but if you stay on top of everything and know your Cavachon well, you can help by catching it early and seeking veterinary attention as soon as you even suspect anything. While there isn't a cure, we can stem the tide and improve quality of life and life expectancy if it is caught early enough.

Symptoms include:

Lumps

Swelling

Sudden weight loss or gain

Skin infections

Loss of appetite or dramatic increase in appetite

Bloody stool

Lethargy

Vomiting

Conjunctivitis

This is one of the most common eye problems for dogs. My first dog went blind because of an eye infection. She lived to the ripe old age of 15, but if her first owner had treated her eye infection, her quality of life would have been better. Conjunctivitis is a horrid swelling of the membrane that covers the back of the eyelids. Conjunctivitis is often brought on by an underlying infection and needs to be seen by a vet.

Symptoms include:

Redness in the eye

Swollen eyelids

Crusty eyes

Persistent squinting

Runny eyes

Lots of blinking

Puppies and weak or ill dogs are far more likely to contract conjunctivitis than healthy adult dogs, as it is an eye infection and so stronger animals can fight it off.

Your vet will be able to prescribe eye drops to help fight off the infection. You need to go to the vet with conjunctivitis as it could be a sign of a different underlying problem and it's not very comfortable so the sooner doggy starts feeling better the better.

Kidney disease

With small dogs such as Cavachons, there is a higher risk of kidney or renal failure, which involves the breakdown of the kidneys, which regulate blood and water levels, and filter and process waste.

Kidney failure is most common in older dogs and is often a natural part of the aging process. The kidneys begin to deteriorate and lose their ability to properly remove waste from the blood stream.

Symptoms include:

Struggling to urinate

Stronger smelling urine

Diarrhoea

Bad breath- smelling like pee

Increased thirst

Lethargy

Weakness

Weight loss

Reduced appetite

Vomiting

If you notice any of these things SEEK IMMEDIATE VETERINARY HELP as catching kidney disease early can help slow down the progression of this horrid illness.

Chronic renal failure (CRF) stems from the gradual deterioration of the tiny units called nephrons, which deal with all the waste and maintain hydration. By time your dog is exhibiting any symptoms, the damage done already to the body in general, kidneys and other organs is usually irreversible. Extreme thirst and frequent urination are among the signs of CRF, along with drooling, dehydration, weight loss and bad breath. Although

CRF is incurable and progressive, a dog can be kept comfortable with dietary changes supervised by your vet, along with IV fluids and specific medications.

Some experts believe that CRF is caused by poor-quality nutrition. Because it occurs gradually, dogs may show no signs for years.

Acute renal failure will transpire quickly, usually from accidental ingestion of a poisonous substance, or illnesses that affect the kidney area. The main thing to remember with kidney disease is that as soon as symptoms are present it is a medical emergency.

There is no cure for renal failure but your veterinarian may be able to suggest things to help you prolong your dog's life. Common management techniques include an IV drip or even a dialysis machine. This special machine can help your pet filter the toxins but this can also be very expensive and you need to be thinking about the long-term quality of life rather than keeping your dog alive as long as possible.

Diabetes

Any mammal can develop diabetes. Diabetes is a condition whereby the insulin that regulates the amount of sugars in the blood is released at the wrong levels, either too much, making blood sugars dangerously low, or too little, making blood sugars dangerously high.

Symptoms include:

Increased appetite without weight gain

Weight loss

Increased thirst

More frequent urination

Weakness

Vomiting

147

Lethargy

If you notice any of these things SEEK IMMEDIATE VETERINARY ADVICE.

Your vet will run both blood and urine tests to screen your dog for diabetes. If your dog is diabetic there are a number of things that can be done. While there is no cure for diabetes it is a very manageable condition. By making adjustments to diet and lifestyle, some diabetic dogs need no further intervention than regular check ups. Other dogs will need daily injections of insulin. This can be a real drain, but if you combine the injections with a treat, the routine will soon become a pleasant one.

Hyperthyroidism

Hyperthyroidism in little dogs is much more common than you'd think. It occurs when the thyroid gland produces too much of the hormone thyroxin, usually in senior dogs. Thyroxin is a hormone that regulates metabolism and too much can cause serious organ damage as it speeds everything up and the animal ages internally much more quickly than they otherwise would. Hyperthyroidism is a condition where one or both of the thyroids become overactive. This over-activity causes a dog's metabolism to rapidly increase, leading to anorexia, kidney failure, serious heart problems and other issues.

Symptoms include:

Increased appetite

Rapid weight loss

Increased thirst

More frequent urination

Vomiting

Lethargy

If you notice any of these things SEEK IMMEDIATE VETERINARY HELP as untreated hyperthyroidism can kill.

There are a number of treatments available, and they are the same as the treatments for hyperthyroidism in humans. There is a medication option. Methimazole is used to counteract the thyroxin. This is not a long-term solution as it needs to be administered daily and is not a substance that naturally occurs in dogs. The next option is thyroid reduction surgery, where the thyroid has a bit literally cut away to make it less efficient. This is a long-term solution and can fix the problem completely, though the risk of surgery usually means your vet will recommend the third option. This is a radioiodine treatment. This is where the animal is given some radioactive iodine, which is attracted to the thyroid and kills part of it off. My mother had this done when her hyperactive thyroid became dangerous. It's non-invasive, much safer than surgery and returns more than 95% of treated dogs to normal thyroid function with no further treatment or medication required. The last 2 options could end up removing too much of the thyroid, in which case synthetic thyroxin can be administered, which is much safer for your animals than Methimazole.

You can reduce the risks involved with hyperthyroidism by seeing your vet regularly.

Obesity

There is an epidemic of overweight dogs. Even fluffy little lambkins like Cavachons should have a waistline. You should be able to feel a waist under the coat. The best ways to avoid obesity are to keep track of what is fed and what is actually eaten. If there is more than one person feeding the dog, or if they beg/steal scraps at the table, then it is a very good idea to keep a record of feeding and eating in your logbook – if they've helped themselves to something of yours then you need to make note of it and feed a little less. If you leave dry food down for your dog to pick at all day be aware of how much is actually eaten.

149

Wet dog food is typically a better food choice for a dog who's getting a little fat, as they are lower in carbohydrates than dry food and more of the food is water, so the dog will feel fuller after taking in less actual food. If your dog will only eat dry food, choose one that is high in protein and low in carbs, and feed measured amounts morning and night rather than free feeding.

If your dog is already obese, consult your vet about a weight loss program and make sure the dog is exercising enough.

Many common dog diseases and health problems are related - directly and indirectly - to obesity, so keeping your dog slim and fit will ensure better overall health and lower vet bills.

Exercise is the key to weight loss, just like with us – weight equals calories burned minus calories taken in. Extended activity play, chase games and puzzles will help you to get your little guy or girl get back into shape.

Dogs can also get mites, lice and worms

A heavy parasite burden can cause serious anaemia and with dogs this can be fatal much quicker than with larger animals. Even if your dog survives a serious parasite burden, they could be left with some pretty horrific health problems as a result of organ damage. This is easily avoided, however, with the correct, regular preventative treatment and observation.

Mites, lice, ticks and other external parasites can be kept in check with regular grooming.

Pale strings in the poop, an increased appetite, weight loss and diarrhoea are all signs of infestation. A large build up of roundworms can be fatal for puppies.

Dogs get tapeworm. These are long and ribbon-shaped and again, horrid. They get this from ingesting a flea that has consumed tapeworm eggs. They hatch in the gut and stomach, attaching themselves to the small intestines. Tapeworms sap nutrients; a dog with a heavy tapeworm burden will lose weight and suffer diarrhoea. As Cavachons are only little, a heavy tapeworm burden can make them seriously ill very quickly.

You can avoid this problem by making sure you're up to date with your de-wormer and flee treatments. Even the cleanest animals can get fleas.

4. Breed specific illnesses

There are a number of breed specific illnesses that a Cavachon may be prone to.

Syringomyelia

Syringomyelia is a disorder of the brain and spinal cord, which may cause severe head and neck pain and possible paralysis. The Cavachon gets this from their King Charles Cavalier background. It is a cluster of cysts on the spinal cord and in the spinal cavity. Symptoms include:

Hypersensitivity in the neck area

Uncontrolled scratching at the neck and shoulders

Air scratching

Weakness in the legs

Holding the head up high even for sleeping and eating

Expressions of pain

The treatment for this condition is a management one. Managing the pain is really the only way to improve the quality of life for the animals involved. There is a surgery, though spinal and neuro surgery on such a small animal is both dangerous and expensive, and the results aren't always positive.

If you suspect Syringomyelia, take your dog to the vet as soon as you can. They will be in pain and need pain medications.

Chronic pancreatitis

Another horrid illness the Cavachon seems prone to is chronic pancreatitis, according to several recent reports. When a pancreas is functioning as it should, the pancreas is protected from early activation of the caustic digestive enzymes, which could result in digesting the pancreas itself. Pancreatitis occurs when the enzymes are activated while still in the pancreas, thereby causing death to its tissue by auto-digestion. Chronic pancreatitis, for which the cavalier appears predisposed and is at an increased risk, is a continuous inflammation that can cause permanent damage to the pancreas. This can lead to diabetes.

Symptoms include:

Abdominal pain

Vomiting

Loss of appetite

Diarrhoea

Blood or mucus in the faeces

Once the cause has been determined and treated, the symptoms will be treated with antiemetics for the acid and pain relief.

MMM

Another hereditary Cavalier problem is called MMM. That stands for Masticatory muscle myositis. It's a form of lockjaw caused by an immune over reaction to illness. This can restrict the movement of the jaw and is very painful.

Symptoms include:

Difficulty opening the mouth

Sensitivity around the mouth

Weight loss

Treatment is best as early as possible. Treatment of this is a series of corticosteroids.

Retinal Dysplasia

The most serious eye defects that afflict high percentages of cavaliers are forms of retinal dysplasia. Retinal dysplasia is a malformation of the retina. It occurs when the two layers of the retina do not form together properly. Mild dysplasia appears as "folds" in the inner retinal layer, called retinal folds.

Symptoms include:

Cloudiness in the eyes

Blindness

The treatment is surgery, though this isn't usually advised or even necessary as the dysplasia doesn't usually develop into blindness and will often stop developing after puppyhood.

This is a genetic condition. Ask your breeder about any family history of retinal dysplasia.

Patellar luxation

Luxating patellas – floating kneecaps – affects 20% of Cavaliers and is almost as common in Bichon Frises. If the condition is not corrected, it will degenerate: the patella's ridges will wear, its groove in the femur will become shallower, and the cavalier will become progressively lamer. Arthritis will prematurely affect the joint, causing a permanently swollen knee with poor mobility. This condition is like patella femeral mal-tracking in humans and let me tell you it is so painful!

Symptoms include:

Swelling around the knees

Hot knees

Pain reactions

Lameness

Unwillingness to walk

The treatment is pain control, anti-inflammatories and eventually surgery. The sooner this is caught the better.

AIHA

Bichon Frises are prone to something called Autoimmune Haemolytic Anaemia or AIHA. This is a condition that sees the dog's immune system attack its own red blood cells, causing anaemia. AIHA in a Bichon Frise can lead to severe anaemia and can be fatal.

Symptoms include:

Weakness

Lack of appetite

Increased heart rate

Pale lips and gums

If you believe your Cavachon suffers from AIHA you should consult a vet immediately. They may prescribe a dose of steroid therapy or another treatment to try to boost the number of red blood cells.

ITP

This is another breed-related problem of the Bichon Frise and therefore the Cavachon, which often accompanies AIHA. It is called Immune-Mediated Thrombocytopenia, often known as Idiopathic Thrombocytopenic Purpura (ITP). ITP is where the clotting platelets in the blood are damaged or destroyed. Platelets assist blood clots in the case of cuts and bruises, so a lack of these will result in symptoms that include haemorrhages of the skin and nosebleeds. In more severe cases you may see blood in a dog's urine and faeces. If you suspect that your dog has ITP you should consult your veterinarian immediately, who may prescribe a dose of steroids or other drugs to combat this health problem.

Allergies

Cavachons are prone to allergies, especially during the spring and summer.

Symptoms include:

Redness around the eyes

Increased scratching and itching

Sneezing

Runny eyes/ nose

Laboured breathing

The best way to treat it is to consult the veterinarian; a well-known vet could be the most invaluable resource when anyone has a dog. The veterinarian will usually prescribe the proper medication in the form of an antihistamine. Always have this on hand but never give it to a dog without veterinary recommendation.

You can avoid allergy problems by keeping on top of dust and other allergen levels in the house.

Kidney stones

This is when waste that has not been properly excreted builds up in the urethra, making urination painful. The longer you leave this, the worse it gets and the more drastic the treatment. Eating too much food that the dog can't digest causes kidney stones. This is another reason not to just feed them your leftovers – they can't always digest human food.

Symptoms include:

Reluctance to urinate

Aggression when urinating

Blood in the urine

The treatment for kidney stones is usually a course of medication if you catch it early enough. If your dog develops very bad kidney stones, surgery can be required. With little dogs like these you want to avoid unnecessary surgery, as they are even more at risk when using anaesthesia.

5. When to go to the vet

It is important to know when to take your dog to see your vet. Early intervention with any illness massively increases the chances of a full recovery or a positive outcome. The main thing to remember is that you know your dog. If you feel like something is off then you should go and see your vet. Trust your instincts. If you want a little more guidance then you can use the list of health problems above; if you suspect any of them the go and find a vet. If you want a tick list then here you go.

If any of the following symptoms appear together or for more than 2 days seek veterinary advice:

Vomiting

Lethargy

Increased urination

Decreased urination

Discoloured urine

Smellier than usual urine

Blood in the urine

Thicker urine

Increased thirst

Decreased thirst

Sudden weight loss

Sudden weight gain

Increased appetite

Decreased appetite

Ingestion of unknown substances

Ingestion of poisonous substances

Fur loss

Loss of fur condition

Yellowing in the gums

Redness of the gums

Any tenderness anywhere

Gunk in the eyes

Runny eyes

Redness around the eyes

Runny nose

Cough

Trying and failing to bring up a hairball

Diarrhoea

With the following things, go to the vet immediately, don't wait a couple of days and don't worry if there are no other symptoms present:

Infected cuts or abscesses

An accident or fall

Ingestion of anything poisonous

You just have an uncomfortable feeling something's not right

The key to good long-term health is to avoid anything going wrong in the first place. There are a number of things you can do about this.

The most obvious thing is to get your dog vaccinated and to keep on top of vaccinations.

This means talking to your vet about what vaccinations are available and setting up a schedule. It's a good idea to keep a record of this in your logbook to make sure that everyone who's involved with your dog is aware of where things are up to.

By getting your Cavachon spayed or neutered you can avoid a myriad of problems. It reduces aggression and the likelihood of fighting. It reduces the urge to wander into unfamiliar territories and get lost, frightened and hit by cars. On a simple, practical level it reduces the number of organs that can have problems. No reproductive organs means no reproductive cancer, as a vet friend of mine puts it "If you ain't got 'em they can't cause problems."

6. Emergency kit

There are a few things you should have on hand with any pet. With most pets you can get the things you'll need in an emergency quite readily at a local store or super market. However, an emergency will often need immediate first aid before you can get to a vet and having everything already on hand so that you don't have to nip out to buy these things can be very useful. An animal first aid kit is an old idea, but a good one.

Styptic

Styptic is a clotting agent used by all sorts of people for all sorts of reasons. Men use it when they cut themselves shaving; rabbit owners use it when they cut the claws too short. When sprinkled on small cuts that bleed for too long, styptic is a fantastic clotting aid and can help a wound heel quickly, avoiding infection. It comes in stick form for human use, but is also available as a powder, such as Kwik-Stop Styptic Powder and works out at about $10 or £7 an ounce. Most dog owners won't use anywhere near that in an animals lifetime.

Antiseptic

An antiseptic gel like Radiol B-R antibacterial Jelly or a spray like Purple Spray can help avoid all sorts of problems. Applied directly and immediately to any minor cuts, scrapes and grazes, an anti-bacterial agent can stop infections occurring, potentially saving hundreds, if not thousands in veterinary bills, as well as a lot of pain and distress for your dog. Even the nicest dog can nip and get nipped. Cavachons are adventurous little things. They have a habit of getting into the bushes and can get into all sorts of scrapes. Any infections should be treated immediately by the vet to avoid septicaemia, and any real wounds need to be looked at by a vet anyway.

Electrolyte compound

Keeping a compound of electrolytes handy could well save your dog's life if they ever develop any diarrhoea or dehydration. If there is ever any point at which your dog is ill, they could easily become dehydrated and die of dehydration rather than the initial illness. Electrolyte compounds such as Macrogol or Replace by Sharps are readily available on eBay and at many pet shops.

7. Logbook

As an animal owner and enthusiast for all things organised, I go on and on about logbooks. A logbook or some sort of general record may well save your dog's life one day. It can make everything easier in the long run too.

For many dog owners a logbook may seem completely over the top in the way of being organised, but for many others, it can literally be a lifesaver. It may seem like a dog's a dog and it's as simple as that, but by keeping precise records that can be accessed and understood by anyone who might require information about your dog's habits, behaviour, feeding and medications, you will be keeping your dog safe, even if you are not the only one to be looking after them. It can mean your vet may be able to pinpoint the sources or beginning of any illnesses.

The back pages should be a calendar, with dates not days, where you can mark on the worming, flea treatment and vaccine dates.

If you do these things to a strict routine, then there will be far less problems of overlap or missing them out. This is also very useful if there are two or more people involved in the care of the animal. Keeping a record of any medical intervention is very handy too, and knowing when exactly they are administered can help to identify bad interactions.

The front pages should contain a list of useful phone numbers (vet, insurance details etc), any regular medications the animal is taking and their description/ microchip information. This can be very useful in case there are any problems when someone else is watching your dog, for example when you are on holiday.

Internal pages should be a week or 2 per page. You should record feed given, any changes in the movement/gait of the dog, interactions with other animals etc. You should also make a record of any time your dog is in transit and how they react to this. If they are ever weighed or measured, you should write this down. If they don't seem to have been eating or drinking this should also be noted.

Chapter 10) Walking with your dog

Walking with your Cavachon is one of the most important things you can do to bond with them. It also helps you to keep their physical and mental health in good condition. There are lots of different things to think about when walking your dog. The type of lead or leash and collar that you use does depend on the breed. Cavachons are not big dogs, and need their walk time and distance to reflect that. They are very playful, though, and so they like games to play along the way. Cavachons, like all dogs, need routine, and a regular walk can help to reinforce the comfort that comes from having a routine. It's very good for your dog to meet other dogs on walks, and if you can walk your dog properly and introduce them to other dogs in the correct way, your dog will really get a kick out of the size and power of the extended pack. One fear a lot of people have about walking a little dog like a Cavachon is aggression from other dogs. The other fear people have is that their dog will be aggressive towards other dogs. If you know how dogs play with each other then you know what is acceptable, and what doesn't require correction.

Cavachons can become distracted from the walk very easily, and it's your job to keep them in check.

Your dog should walk beside or behind you with your arms relaxed by your side with no tension on the lead unless you're correcting behaviour. If you need to correct unwanted behaviour while your dog is on the lead you can give a quick snap up with the lead. Your dog should always be concentrating on the walk or on you, not on other dogs or on other interesting things out in the world. Don't let them start looking at cars or cats. You need to let the dog know where a good place to "go" is by stopping there, maybe pause in the same place as the dog went yesterday, but you mustn't let them pee on every tree.

The type of collar and lead you choose is completely your choice, but there are a few things you should keep in mind. Cavachons

161

are medium to small dogs. They don't have the power to need a choke chain or a slip lead. There isn't really much justification for using these types of leads unless you have a big, aggressive or dominant dog. Cavachons don't need a harness. Harnesses encourage pulling and are not really needed for medium to small dogs. Harnesses are for large dogs to pull sleds or for very small or elderly medium dogs so that they don't get hurt. A high collar and a lead are ideal for this size of dog and there is nothing for the longer fur of the Cavachon to get caught or pinched in. They are good for working with your dog in the home, too, as the collar can stay on all of the time, giving you a convenient handle to catch them by.

Cavachons aren't big dogs. The distance for walking a Cavachon is nowhere near the distance you need to walk a big dog like a Great Dane, and they don't need hours of walking every day. A couple of walks at a quarter of an hour each will usually be enough, though a long work at the weekend won't upset them too much. There are some dogs that can't cope with long walks and you do need to be aware of your dog's energy levels. If they are getting tired then it is time to go home as exhaustion can make little dogs sick.

Games like fetch and tug-of-war are great games to play on walks; they get rid of excess energy very quickly by playing and interacting with people in a positive way. Playing games like this mean that the excitement can be used up outside, meaning that your dog will be calmer at home.

Routine is important for any dog, and little Cavachons are no different. They need to know that their home is safe and stable and to know what it expected of them. A good routine can really help to reinforce that. You can build your routine around walking. Ideally your dog should be out at least 3 times a day, and at least 2 of those times should be for a walk, even 10 minutes round the block will do. The specifics of your walking routine are up to you, but you need to make sure your dog is in a calm, submissive state before you leave the house. If they get excited while you're getting ready, send them away until you're ready. If they get excited while you get the lead on, make them calm down before you carry on. Don't let them go through the door before you, you are in charge. This puts them in a good state of mind to begin with.

1. Other dogs

Intact (non-neutered) males and females are more likely to display aggression related to sexual behaviour than neutered animals are. Fighting, particularly in males, that is directed at other males is less common after neutering.
The intensity of other types of aggression, such as irritable aggression in females will be totally eliminated by spaying.

Aggressive dogs on a walk can make you very worried and your fear will be projected onto your dog, making them either frightened or aggressive to protect you. This will not only potentially get your dog hurt, but will also undermine your position as pack leader. If a dog is behaving aggressively towards your dog and straining on their lead to get to your dog, you need to claim your dog. You are pack leader. Stand in front of your dog, keeping them calm and submissive, and claiming the space around you and your dog. Don't talk to the other dog, just stay calm and assertive. Say hi to the other owner, "hi, what's his/her name? You guys having a good walk?" This is a conversation pack leader to pack leader and will usually calm the situation. If you are very nervous of other dogs you can walk with a long walking stick, like a staff, but never raise it above other dogs, as this can aggravate a situation, but you can use it to block.

Your dog's aggression can be an absolutely heartbreaking situation. It is mortifying to see your dog displaying any signs of aggression whatsoever. It makes you less likely to walk them; it makes you less confident of your own dog. You can avoid this by letting your dog know you are going to protect them by walking your dog beside or behind you and correcting over excited behaviour before it develops into aggression. Any dominant behaviour, like putting paws or head on top of other dogs, should be corrected immediately and your dog won't ever get to a state where they are aggressive. Keep claiming your dog and your space. You being the boss lets your dog relax and be happy or calm.

It is important to be able to recognise normal greeting and play behaviour. Dogs should sniff each other's rear end to introduce themselves. The tail shouldn't be too high and assertive, but shouldn't be between the legs, as this is a fear response and will encourage other dogs to dominate them. If one dog drops their front to their elbows, this is an invitation to play and then they will probably play a chase or dance game. It helps if you and the other owner can have a little chat – it shows that the two packs are friends. Friendly dogs playing together is a lovely sight.

2. Dealing with aggression and fights

As a dog owner you will want to know how to deal with other dogs when you're out on a walk. There will be some times when you'll come across over excited or aggressive dogs. Now it's time to stand your ground. Here, to avoid a confrontation, you need to prove to your dog, and to the other dog, that you are in charge. The way to do this is to remain calm. Exert calm, assertive energy. Stand up right and still in front of your dog - claiming them - and keep assertive. Don't talk to the strange dog and keep your hands by your side and close to your body. Running away can reinforce the dog's prey instinct to chase and catch animals - including you and your dog, and he may pursue you vigorously even if its initial intent was just playful. In addition, you won't be able to outrun a dog if you're on foot but your dog will become agitated and fight the other dog. Don't make it defend you. If the other dog's owners aren't about you should maintain your position, turning sideways to the dog and keeping it in your peripheral vision instead of facing him and making eye contact. This will signal to the dog that you are not a threat but that you aren't prey either. Don't open your hands and arms up to a bite by extending them. Keep your fingers curled into fists to avoid getting them bitten. The dog may come quite close, even sniffing you, without actually biting. Standing side on allows the dog to come to smell you and calm down. Once the dog is calm you can let your dog smell the other dog. The other dog at this point should have been taken away or joined by an owner. If not you can send them away, once they have calmed down. If the other dog does bite or attack you, you need to stay calm and fight back. A dog attack can be fatal so bash it with a stick if you have one with you.

If you or your dog is bitten you still need to stay calm.

Excitement at this point will only make it worse. A calm shout in a deep voice will do. If the dog that is biting, at this point it could be either, doesn't let go, don't pull. This will cause a reaction, reinforcing the bite instinct and can also make the bite tear. What you should do is hold the biting dog still and pry the jaws open. Seek immediate veterinary or medical attention. Call the authorities. Dogs that bite need to be reported and dealt with.

Chapter 11) Breeding

Not spaying a dog and breeding her a lot means she is very likely to get mammary cancer. Not neutering a male dog can lead to all manner of behavioural issues. It causes frustration and aggression. Breeding more dogs contributes to the overall dog population. Too many dogs means that more dogs end up in the pound or in shelters. If you choose to breed your dog you need to be prepared to take responsibility for the long-term health and wellbeing of your own dog and of any resulting puppies. It's your fault the puppies exist. You have to make sure they are safe and healthy. If the new owners can't look after the puppies, do you want them to go to a shelter? Can you afford to look after any rejected dogs? Can you afford any unexpected veterinary bills that arise from breeding your dog? Keep in mind that breeding and breeding-related problems usually aren't covered by your insurance.

Why do you want to breed?

Any responsible breeder will tell you that it is no way to make a fast buck. The amount of time, effort and potential expense is huge. The specific nutrition a pregnant mother needs, then a nursing mother, and then the puppies will hugely increase your food bill. There is so much hard work involved in breeding that you really need to be sure of why you are doing it. The only reason to breed from your pet – unless you are already a breeder and know what you're doing – is that you love her and want another dog with her personality. The stress, worry and occasional heartbreak involved in breeding would lead me to advise against it. Cavachons are little dogs that have larger litters, which can cause all sorts of complications. If you decide to breed from your dog, despite the warnings, I'll give you as much information as I can to make it as safe and positive as possible. You should also contact other breeders for help and information. Dog breeders are generally great people, and they care primarily about the wellbeing of the dogs. They will advise you not to breed, but will tell you what you need to know. The best way to breed from your dog is to take her to a stud at a breeder's house. They will usually be there for you if anything goes wrong.

Don't breed your dog too young. While she'll come into heat at about 6 months, her body isn't done growing yet. She shouldn't be bred under the age of about one and a half to two. By this age she is strong enough to cope with the rigors of pregnancy, birth and nursing. Have her checked over by a vet to make sure she is strong enough.

Mating

Mating can be a dangerous time for any animal, but for dogs you need to be very careful. If you are breeding your female you will usually use a stud male. This controlled breeding situation is much safer than mating with some random dog from the park. It is important to think about the re-homing of the puppies when choosing the male to mate your female to; it will help if the male is Cavachon, Bichon Frise or King Charles Cavalier. If you find a professional stud, they will be able to talk you through the process and supervise everything to make sure it is safe.

Pregnancy

She will be pregnant for 63 days.

Pregnancy food

Your pregnant dog needs a lot more high quality nutrition. Your vet will be able to recommend specific vitamin supplements for your pregnant dog. The food should be a complete dog food, both dry and wet. DON'T give calcium supplements during pregnancy. It's not good for her and can make the birth dangerous. You can give calcium during labour. Calcium during the pushing stage of labour will make the muscles contract at that specific moment. You can give a multivitamin and half an egg a day to help keep her condition up.

Pregnancy care

Mum needs exercise while she's expecting, but you need to be very aware of her energy levels. If she starts to flag, let her go to bed as soon as possible. Make sure she is always warm enough or cool enough and comfortable. She should know that she is safe around you and around the home. She may become aggressive towards other dogs during her pregnancy. Try to make sure she can get away from other animals and any children in the house. About ten days before the birth mum needs to be getting used to her whelping box. The whelping box needs to be a square about one and a half times as long as she is, and as tall as she is. This will give room for her to move about with the puppies and to get out of the box, but will keep the puppies in there safe.

1. Puppies with mum

After the birth she can have puppy foods and additional calcium to help the uterus contract properly. Mum needs to know that her babies are safe. This will mean that she needs to know where other animals and people in the house are. She may snap at other animals approaching the puppies and mustn't be punished for this – she's protecting her babies.

Puppies can't regulate their own temperature, so mum needs to be able to warm them up and cool them down. She'll cool them down by pushing them away from her and warm them up by moving them towards her. The whelping box needs to be big enough for her to be able to do this.

Mum will feed the babies whenever they need feeding, but you need to make sure that none of her mammary glands are hard or infected, as mastitis can be really painful or even dangerous.

The puppies will begin to eat solid food when they are ready and mum will supervise this. The puppies will be fully weaned by about 6 weeks, but shouldn't be separated from mum and siblings until they are at least 8 weeks.

2. Puppies without mum

Sometimes, mum won't be able to look after all of the puppies. It is likely that any puppies that mum can't look after will die. However well you do looking after any puppies, you will probably end up heartbroken. Before there are any puppies on the scene, you should find out about other dogs that will have puppies at about the same time. This way you may be able to find a foster mum for any abandoned or orphaned puppies. If this isn't an option you may have to hand rear. Hand reared dogs may seem like a great idea, but the reality is that they often make nightmare pets. I cannot stress enough how important it is for you to avoid having to hand rear any puppies. If you have to, here's what you do:

Puppies can't regulate their own temperature, so you need to do that for them, giving them a bed with a small heat mat under half of it will allow them to move from cooler or warmer as they need.

Find a bottle with a newborn nipple; pet hand rearing bottles have nipples that are too small and narrow for puppies.

Most vets carry puppy replacer milk, or you can use goats milk which you can find in most supermarkets. DO NOT GIVE COWS MILK as this can cause fatal diarrhoea and dehydration. There are lots of sites that say you can boil cows milk and make it safe for puppies – you can't. Boiling something doesn't change its content. The large fat molecules and the sugars in cow's milk irritate the stomach and intestines of dogs and in very young puppies this can be fatal. Newborn puppies need to be bottle-fed EVERY 2 to 3 HOURS. Never feed a cold puppy, make sure they are warm enough by having a little cuddle with them and checking the ears and tail – they should never feel cold. Newborn puppies have tiny stomachs and cannot close their throats, so if you fill up the stomach and throat, the milk will just run into their lungs and drown them. Never feed them on their back. This can also drown them. Feed them on their bellies or on their side.

They don't pee or poop without mum licking them around their genitals, this is to keep their nest clean. If the mother isn't able to do it, you have to clean it. Take a warm, damp washcloth and wipe their backside and that whole area to make them do their business. Once they start learning to walk, they will be able to "go" on their own and will not need your assistance any more.

The puppies will be able to eat from a few weeks old, but should still have access to milk until they are about 6 weeks old. From then on you need to help them to learn how to behave. Don't re-home/sell the puppies until they are 8-weeks-old – they are too young to be separated.

3. Finding homes

Your next responsibility is to find homes for all the little ones. You can advertise on breed specific forums and websites, or speak to local breeders for advice. You have to find responsible, knowledgeable homes and people who have done the proper research. They should know as much as you knew before embarking on this little adventure.

You can place adverts online and with your original breeder. Make sure your puppies are going to be well looked after in their new life, as they are your responsibility. You literally made them exist. Be very circumspect as to potential buyers and make sure you do your checks on the owner – you don't want them to go to neglectful, unknowledgeable, abusive or puppy faming homes.

Chapter 12) Poisonous foods and plants

1. Poisonous Foods

While some dogs are smart enough not to want to eat foods that can harm or kill them, other canine companions will eat absolutely anything they can get their teeth into.

As conscientious guardians for our fur friends, it will always be our responsibility to make certain that when we share our homes with a dog, we never leave foods that could be toxic or lethal to them easily within their reach.

While there are many foods that can be toxic to a Cavachon, the following alphabetical list contains some of the more common foods that can seriously harm or even kill our dogs including:

Bread Dough: if your dog eats bread dough, their body heat will cause the dough to rise inside the stomach. As the dough expands during the rising process, alcohol is produced.

Dogs who have eaten bread dough may experience stomach bloating, abdominal pain, vomiting, disorientation and depression. Because bread dough can rise to many times its size, eating only a small amount will cause a problem for any dog.

Broccoli: the toxic ingredient in broccoli is isothiocynate. While it may cause stomach upset, it probably won't be very harmful unless the amount eaten is more than 10% of the dog's total daily diet.

Chocolate: contains theobromine, a chemical that is toxic to dogs in large enough quantities. Chocolate also contains caffeine, which is found in coffee, tea, and certain soft drinks. Different types of chocolate contain different amounts of theobromine and caffeine.

For example, dark chocolate and baking chocolate or cocoa powder contain more of these compounds than milk chocolate does, therefore, a dog would need to eat more milk chocolate in order to become ill.

However, even a few ounces of chocolate can be enough to cause illness or death in a small dog like the Cavachon, therefore, no amount or type of chocolate should be considered safe for a dog to eat.

Chocolate toxicity can cause vomiting, diarrhoea, rapid or irregular heart rate, restlessness, muscle tremors, and seizures. Death can occur within 24 hours of eating.

During many holidays such as Christmas, New Year's, Valentine's, Easter and Halloween, chocolate is often more easily accessible to curious dogs, especially from children who are not so careful with where they keep their Halloween stash and who are an easy mark for a hungry dog.

In some cases, people unwittingly poison their dogs by offering them chocolate as a treat or leaving a luscious chocolate frosted cake easily within licking distance when nobody is looking.

Caffeine: beverages containing caffeine (like soda, tea, coffee, chocolate) act as a stimulant and can accelerate your dog's heartbeat to a dangerous level. Dogs eating caffeine have been known to have seizures, some of which are fatal.

Cooked Bones: can be extremely hazardous for a dog because the bones become brittle when cooked which causes them to splinter when the dog chews on them.

The splinters have sharp edges that have been known to become stuck in the teeth, and cause choking when caught in the throat or cause a rupture or puncture of the stomach lining or intestinal tract.

Especially dangerous are cooked turkey and chicken legs, ham, pork chop and veal bones. Symptoms of choking include:

- Pale or blue gums
- Gasping open-mouthed breathing
- Pawing at the face
- Slow, shallow breathing
- Unconscious, with dilated pupils

Grapes and Raisins: can cause acute (sudden) kidney failure in dogs. While it is unknown what the toxic agent is in this fruit, clinical signs can occur within 24 hours of eating and include vomiting, diarrhoea, and lethargy (tiredness).

Other signs of illness caused from eating grapes or raisins relate to the eventual shutdown of kidney functioning.

Garlic and Onions: contain chemicals that damage red blood cells by rupturing them so that they lose their ability to carry oxygen effectively, which leave the dog short of oxygen, causing what is called *"hemolytic anemia"*.

Poisoning can occur with a single ingestion of large quantities of garlic or onions or with repeated meals containing small amounts.

Cooking does not reduce the potential toxicity of onions and garlic.

NOTE: fresh, cooked, and/or powdered garlic or onions are commonly found in baby food, which is sometimes given to dogs when they are sick, therefore, be certain to carefully read food labels before feeding to your Cavachon.

Macadamia Nuts: are commonly found in candies and chocolates. Although the mechanism of macadamia nut toxicity is not well understood, the clinical signs in dogs having eaten these nuts include depression, weakness, vomiting, tremors, joint pain, and pale gums.

Signs can occur within 12 hours after eating. In some cases, symptoms can resolve themselves without treatment within 24 to 48 hours, however, keeping a close eye on your Cavachon will be strongly recommended.

Mushrooms: mushroom poisoning can be fatal if certain species of mushrooms are eaten.

The most commonly reported severely toxic species of mushroom in the US is Amanita phalloides (Death Cap mushroom), which is also quite a common species found in most parts of Britain. Other Amanita species are also toxic.

This deadly mushroom is often found growing in grassy or wooded area near various deciduous and coniferous trees, which means that if you're out walking with your Cavachon in the woods, they could easily find these mushrooms.

Eating them can cause severe liver disease and neurological disorders. If you suspect your dog has eaten these mushrooms, immediately take them to your veterinarian, as the recommended treatment is to induce vomiting and to give activated charcoal. Further treatment for liver disease may also be necessary.

Pits and Seeds: many seeds and pits found in a variety of fruits, including apples, apricots, cherries, pears and plums, contain cyanogenic glycosides that can cause cyanide poisoning in your Cavachon.

The symptoms of cyanide poisoning usually occur within 15-20 minutes to a few hours after eating and symptoms can include initial excitement, followed by rapid respiration rate, salivation, voiding of urine and faeces, vomiting, muscle spasm, staggering, and coma before death.

Dogs suffering from cyanide poisoning that live more than 2 hours after the onset of symptoms will usually recover.

Raw Salmon or Trout: Salmon Poisoning Disease (SPD) can be a problem for anyone who feeds their dog a raw meat diet that includes raw salmon or trout. The cause is infection by a rickettsial organism called Neorickettsia helminthoeca.

Nanophyteus salmincola are found to infect some species of freshwater snails. The infected snail is eaten by the fish as part of the food chain. The dog is exposed only when it eats an infected fish.

A sudden onset of symptoms occurs 5-7 days after eating the infected fish. In the acute stages, gastrointestinal symptoms are quite similar to canine parvovirus.

SPD has a mortality rate of up to 90%, can be diagnosed with a faecal sample and is treatable if caught in time.

Prevention is simple, cook all fish before feeding it to your Cavachon and immediately see your veterinarian if you suspect that your dog has eaten raw salmon or trout.

Tobacco: all forms of tobacco, including patches, nicotine gum and chewing tobacco can be fatal to dogs if eaten.

Signs of poisoning can appear within an hour and include hyperactivity, salivation, panting, vomiting and diarrhoea. Advanced signs include muscle weakness, twitching, collapse, coma, increased heart rate and eventually cardiac arrest.

Never leave tobacco products within reach of your Cavachon, and if you suspect your dog has eaten any of these, seek immediate veterinary help.

Tomatoes: contain atropine, which can cause dilated pupils, tremors and irregular heartbeat. The highest concentration of atropine is found in the leaves and stems of tomato plants, next is the unripe (green) tomatoes, followed by the ripe tomato.

Xylitol: is an artificial sweetener found in products such as gum, candy, mints, toothpaste, and mouthwash that is recognized by the National Animal Poison Control Center to be a risk to dogs.

Xylitol is harmful to dogs because it causes a sudden release of insulin in the body that leads to hypoglycemia (low blood sugar). Xylitol can also cause liver damage in dogs.

Within 30 minutes after eating a product containing xylitol, the dog may vomit, be lethargic (tired), and/or be uncoordinated. However, some signs of toxicity can also be delayed for hours or even for a few days. Xylitol toxicity in dogs can be fatal if left untreated.

Please be aware that the above list is just some of the more common foods that can be toxic or fatal to our fur friends and that there are other foods we should never be feeding our dogs.

If you have one of those dogs who will happily eat anything that looks or smells even slightly like food, be certain to keep these foods far away from your beloved Cavachon and you'll help them to live a long and healthy life.

2. Poisonous Household Plants

Many common house plants are actually poisonous to our canine companions, and although many dogs simply will ignore house plants, some will attempt to eat anything, especially puppies who want to taste everything in their new world.

More than 700 plant species contain toxins that may harm or be fatal to puppies or dogs depending on the size of the puppy or dog and how much they may eat. It will be especially important to be aware of the more common household plants when you are sharing your home with a new puppy.

Following is a short list of the more common household plants, what they look like, the different names they are known by, and what symptoms would be apparent if your puppy or dog decides to eat them.

Aloe Plant: (medicine plant or Barbados aloe), is a very common succulent that is toxic to dogs. The toxic agent in this plant is Aloin.

The bitter yellow substance is found in most aloe species and may cause vomiting and/or reddish urine.

Asparagus Fern: (emerald feather, emerald fern, sprengeri fern, plumosa fern, lace fern) The toxic agent in this plant is sapogenin — a steroid found in a variety of plants. Berries of this plant cause vomiting, diarrhoea and/or abdominal pain or (skin inflammation) from repeated exposure.

Corn Plant: (cornstalk plant, dracaena, dragon tree, ribbon plant) is toxic to dogs. Saponin is the offensive chemical compound found in this plant. If the plant is eaten, vomiting (with or without blood), loss of appetite, depression and/or increased salivation can occur.

Cyclamen: (Sowbread) is a pretty, flowering plant that, if eaten, can cause increased salivation, vomiting and diarrhoea. If a dog eats a large amount of the plant's tubers, which are usually found below the soil at the root — heart rhythm abnormalities, seizures and even death can occur.

Dieffenbachia: (dumb cane, tropic snow, exotica) contains a chemical that is a poisonous deterrent to animals. If the plant is eaten, oral irritation can occur, especially on the tongue and lips.

This irritation can lead to increased salivation, difficulty swallowing and vomiting.

Elephant Ear: (caladium, taro, pai, ape, cape, via, via sori, malanga) contains a chemical similar to that found in dieffenbachia, therefore, an dog's toxic reaction to elephant ear is similar: oral irritation, increased salivation, difficulty swallowing and vomiting.

Heartleaf Philodendron: (horsehead philodendron, cordatum, fiddle leaf, panda plant, split-leaf philodendron, fruit salad plant, red emerald, red princess, saddle leaf), is a common, easy-to-grow houseplant that contains a chemical irritating to the mouth, tongue and lips of dogs. An affected dog may also experience

180

increased salivation, vomiting and difficulty swallowing.

JadePlant: (baby jade, dwarf rubber plant, jade tree, Chinese rubber plant, Japanese rubber plant, friendship tree). While the toxic property in this plant is unknown, eating it can cause depression, loss of coordination and, although more rare, slow heart rate.

Lilies: some plants of the lily family are toxic to dogs. The peace lily (also known as Mauna Loa) is toxic to dogs. Eating the peace lily or calla lily can cause irritation of the tongue and lips, increased salivation, difficulty swallowing and vomiting.

Satin Pothos: (silk pothos), if eaten by a dog, the plant may cause irritation to the mouth, lips and tongue, while the dog may also experience increased salivation, vomiting and/or difficulty swallowing.

The plants noted above are only a few of the more common household plants, and every conscientious Cavachon guardian will want to educate themselves before bringing plants into the home that could be toxic to their canine companions.

3. Poison Proof Your Home

You can learn about many potentially toxic and poisonous sources both inside and outside your home by visiting the ASPCA Animal Poison Control Centre website.

Always keep your veterinarian's emergency number in a place where you can quickly access it, as well as the Emergency Poison Control telephone number, in case you suspect that your dog may have been poisoned.

Knowing what to do if you suspect your dog may have been poisoned and being able to quickly contact the right people could save your Cavachon's life.

If you keep toxic cleaning substances (including fertilizers and vehicle products) in your home or garage, always keep them behind closed doors. As well, keep any medications where your Cavachon can never get to them, and seriously consider

183

eliminating the use of any and all toxic products, for the health of both yourself and your best friend.

4. Garden Plants

Please note that there are also many outdoor plants that can be toxic or poisonous to your Cavachon, therefore, always check what plants are growing in your garden and if any may be harmful, remove them or make certain that your Cavachon puppy or adult dog cannot eat them.

Cornell University Department of Animal Science lists many different categories of poisonous plants affecting dogs, including house plants, flower garden plants, vegetable garden plants, plants found in swamps or moist areas, plants found in fields, trees and shrubs, plants found in wooded areas, and ornamental plants.

5. Grass

Also, be aware that many puppies and adult dogs will eat grass, just because. Perhaps they are bored, or need a little fibre in their diet. Remember that canines are natural scavengers, always on the look out for something they can eat, and as long as the grass is healthy and has not been sprayed with toxic chemicals, this should not be a concern.

6. Animal Poison Control Centre

The ASPCA Animal Poison Control Centre is staffed 24 hours a day, 365 days a year and is a valuable resource for learning about what plants are toxic and possibly poisonous to your dog.

Poison Emergency USA

Call: 1 (888) 426-4435
When calling the Poison Emergency number, a $65. US (£39.42) consultation fee may be applied to your credit card.

Poison Emergency UK

- Call Pet Poison Helpline 800-213-6680 (payable service)

- Call RSPCA 0300 1234 999

www.aspca.org = ASPCA Poison Control

Chapter 13) Looking after an older dog.

1. What to Be Aware Of

As a result of advances in veterinarian care, improvements in diet and nutrition and general knowledge concerning the proper care of our canine companions, our dogs are able to enjoy longer, healthier lives, and as such, when caring for them we need to be aware of behavioural and physical changes that will affect our dogs as they approach old age.

A Cavachon will be entering their senior years at around age 8 to 10 years of age.

a) Physiological Changes

As our beloved canine companions become senior dogs, they will be suffering from very similar physical aging problems that affect us humans, such as pain, stiffness and arthritis, diminished or complete loss of hearing and sight and inability to control their bowels and bladder. Any of these problems will reduce a dog's willingness to want to exercise.

b) Behavioural Changes

Further, a senior Cavachon may experience behavioural changes resulting from loss of hearing and sight, such as disorientation, fear or startled reactions and overall grumpiness from any number of physical problems that could be causing them pain whenever they move.

Just as research and science has improved our human quality of life in our senior years, the same is becoming true for our canine counterparts who are able to benefit from dietary supplements and pharmaceutical products to help them be as comfortable as possible in their advancing years.

Of course there will be some inconveniences associated with keeping an older dog around the home, however, your Cavachon deserves no less than to spend their final days in your loving care after they have unconditionally given you their entire lives.

c) Geriatric Dogs

Being aware of the changes that are likely occurring in a senior dog will help you to better care for them during their geriatric years.

For instance, most dogs will experience hearing loss and visual impairment. If a dog's hearing is compromised, then using more hand signals will be helpful.

Deaf dogs will still be able to hear louder noises and feel vibrations, therefore hand clapping, using a loud clicker or stomping your foot on the floor may be a way to get their attention.

If a senior dog loses their eyesight, most dogs will still be able to easily navigate their familiar surroundings, and you will only need to be extra watchful on their behalf when taking them to unfamiliar territory. If they still have their hearing, you will be able to assist your dog with verbal cues and commands.

Dogs that have lost both their hearing and their sight will need to be close to you so that they can relax and not feel nervous, and so that you can communicate by touching parts of their body.

Generally speaking, even when a dog becomes blind and/or deaf, their powerful sense of smell is still functioning, which means that they will be able to tell where you are and navigate their environment by using their nose.

d) More Bathroom Breaks

Bathroom breaks may need to become more frequent in older dogs who may lose their ability to hold it for longer periods of time, so be prepared to be more watchful and to offer them opportunities to go outside more frequently during the day.

You may also want to place a pee pad near the door, in case they just can't hold it long enough, or if you have not already taught them to go on an indoor potty patch, or pee pad, now may be the time for this alternative bathroom arrangement.

A dog who has been house trained for years will feel the shame and upset of not being able to hold it long enough to get to their regular bathroom location, so be kind and do whatever you need to do to help them not to have to feel bad about failing bowel or bladder control.

Our beloved canine companions may also begin to show signs of cognitive decline and changes in the way their brain functions, similar to what happens to humans suffering from Alzheimer's, where they start to wander about aimlessly, sometimes during the middle of the night. Make sure that if this is happening with your Cavachon at night time, they cannot accidentally harm themselves.

Being aware that an aging Cavachon will be experiencing many symptoms that are similar to an aging human will help you to understand how best to keep them safe and as comfortable as possible during this golden age in their lives.

2. How to Make Them Comfortable

a) Regular Checkups

During this time in your Cavachon's life, when their immune systems become weakened and they may be experiencing pain, you will want to get into the habit of taking your senior Cavachon for regular veterinarian check-ups. Take them for a veterinarian check-up every six months so that early detection of any problems can quickly be attended to and solutions for helping to keep your aging Cavachon comfortable can be provided.

b) No Rough Play

An older Cavachon will not have the same energy or willingness to play as they did when they were younger, therefore, do not allow younger children to rough house with an older dog. Explain to them that the dog is getting older and that as a result they must learn to be gentle and to leave the dog alone when it may want to rest or sleep.

c) Mild Exercise

Dogs still love going for walks, even when they are getting older and slowing down. Although an older Cavachon will generally have less energy, they still need to exercise and keep moving, and taking them out regularly for shorter walks will keep them healthier and happier long into old age.

d) Best Quality Food

Everyone has heard the saying, *"you are what you eat"* and for a senior dog, what he or she eats is even more important as his or her digestive system may no longer be functioning at peak performance. Therefore, feeding a high quality, protein-based food will be important for their continued health.

As well, if your older Cavachon is overweight, you will want to help them shed excess pounds so that they will not be placing undue stress on their joints or heart, and the best way to do this is by feeding smaller quantities of a higher quality food.

e) Clean and Parasite Free

The last thing an aging Cavachon should have to deal with is the misery of itching and scratching, so make sure that you continue to give them regular baths with the appropriate shampoos and conditioners to keep their coat and skin comfortable and free from parasites.

f) Plenty of Water

Proper hydration is essential for helping to keep an older Cavachon comfortable. Water is life giving for every creature, so make certain that your aging dog has easy access to plenty of clean, fresh water, which will help to improve their energy and digestion and also prevent dehydration, which can add to joint stiffness.

g) Keeping Warm

Just as older humans feel the cold more, so do older dogs. Keeping your senior Cavachon warm will help to alleviate some of the pain of their joint stiffness or arthritis. Make sure their bed or kennel is not kept in a drafty location and perhaps consider a heated bed for them.

Be aware that your aging Cavachon will be more sensitive to extremes in temperature, and it will be up to you to make sure that they are comfortable at all times, which means not too hot and not too cold.

h) Indoor Clothing

We humans tend to wear warmer clothing as we get older, simply because we have more difficulty maintaining a comfortable body temperature and the same will be true of our senior Cavachon companions.

Therefore, while you most likely already have a selection of outdoor clothing appropriate to the climate in which you live, you may not have considered keeping your Cavachon warm while inside the home. Now would be the time to consider doggy t-shirts or sweater clothing options to help keep your aging companion comfortably warm both inside and outside.

i) Steps or Stairs

If your Cavachon is allowed to sleep on the human couch or chair, but they are having difficulties getting up there as their joints are becoming stiff and painful, consider buying them a set of foam stairs so that they do not have to make the jump to their favourite sleeping place.

j) Comfortable Bed

While most dogs seem to be happy with sleeping on the floor, providing them with a padded, soft bed will greatly help to relieve sore spots and joint pain in older dogs.

If there is a draft in the home, generally it will be at floor level, therefore a bed that is raised up off of the floor will be warmer for your senior Cavachon, who will be much more comfortable sleeping in a cosy dog bed.

k) More Love and Attention

Last, but not least, make sure that you give your senior Cavachon lots of love and attention and never leave them alone for long periods of time.

When they are not feeling their best, they will want to be with you all that much more because you are their guardian whom they trust and love beyond life itself.

3. What is Euthanasia?

Every veterinarian will have received special training to help provide all incurably ill, injured or aged pets that have come to the end of their natural lives with a humane and gentle death, through a process called *"euthanasia"*.

When the time comes, euthanasia, or putting a dog *"to sleep"*, will usually be a two-step process.

Firstly, the veterinarian will inject the dog with a sedative to make them sleepy, calm and comfortable.

Secondly, the veterinarian will inject a special drug that will peacefully stop their heart. These drugs work in such a way that the dog will not experience any awareness whatsoever that their life is ending. What they will experience is very much like what we humans experience when going under anaesthesia during a surgical procedure.

Once the second stage drug has been injected, the entire process takes about 10 to 20 seconds, at which time the veterinarian will then check to make certain that the dog's heart has stopped.

There is no suffering with this process, which is a very gentle and humane way to end a dog's suffering and allow them to peacefully pass on.

4. When to Help a Dog Transition

The impending loss of a beloved dog is one of the most painfully difficult and emotionally devastating coping experiences a canine guardian will ever have to face.

For the sake of our faithful companions, because we do not want to prolong their suffering, we humans will have to do our best to look at our dog's situation practically, rather than emotionally, so that we can make the best decision for them.

They may be suffering from extreme old age and the inability to even walk outside to relieve themselves, and thus suffering the indignity of regularly soiling their sleeping area, or they may have been diagnosed with an incurable illness that is causing them a lot of pain, or they may have been seriously injured.

Whatever the reason for a canine companion's suffering, it will be up to their human guardian to calmly guide the end-of-life experience so that any further discomfort and distress can be minimised.

a) When There is Uncertainty

In circumstances where it is not entirely clear how much a dog is suffering, it will be helpful to pay close attention to your Cavachon's behaviour and keep a daily log or record so that you can know for certain how much of their day is difficult and painful for them, and how much is not.

When you keep a daily log, it will be easier to decide if the dog's quality of life has become so poor that it makes better sense to offer them the gift of peacefully going to sleep or not.
During this time of uncertainty, it will also be very important to discuss with a veterinarian what signs of suffering may be associated with the dog's particular disease or condition, so that you know what to look for.

Often a dog may still continue to eat or drink despite being distraught, having difficulty breathing, excessively panting, being disoriented or in a lot of pain, and as their caring guardians, we will have to weigh their love of eating against how much they are really suffering in all other aspects of their life.

Obviously, if a canine guardian can clearly see that their beloved companion is suffering throughout their days and nights, it will make sense to help humanely end their suffering by planning a euthanasia procedure.

We humans are often tempted to delay the inevitable moment of euthanasia because we love our dogs so much and cannot bear the anticipation of the intense grief we know will overwhelm us when we must say our final goodbyes to our beloved fur friend.

Unfortunately, we may regret that we allowed our dog to suffer too long, and find ourselves wishing that if only we humans had the same option, to peacefully let go, when we reach such a stage in our own lives.

5. Grieving a Lost Pet

Often we humans do not fully recognize the terrible grief involved in losing a beloved canine friend. There will be many who do not understand the close bond we humans can have with our dogs, which is often unlike any we have with our human counterparts.

Your friends may give you pitying looks and try to cheer you up, but if they have never experienced such a loss themselves, they may also secretly think you are making too much fuss over "just a dog".

For some of us humans, the loss of a beloved dog is so painful that they decide never to share their lives with another, because they cannot bear the thought of going through the pain of loss again.

Expect to feel terribly sad, tearful and yes, depressed because those who are close to their canine companions will feel their loss no less acutely than the loss of a human friend or life partner. The grieving process can take some time to recover from, and some of us never totally recover.

After the loss of a family dog, first you need to take care of yourself by making certain that you keep eating and getting regular sleep, even though you will feel an almost eerie sense of loneliness.

Losing a beloved dog is a shock to the system, which can also affect your concentration and your ability to find joy or want to participate in other activities that may be part of the rest of your life.

During this early grieving time you will need to take extra care while driving or performing tasks that require your concentration as you may find yourself distracted.

If there are other dogs or pets in the home, they will also be grieving the loss of a companion, and may display this by acting depressed, being off their food or showing little interest in play or games. Therefore, you need to help guide your other pets through this grieving process by keeping them busy and interested, taking them for extra walks and spending more time with them.

Many people do not wait long enough before attempting to replace a lost pet and will immediately go to the local shelter and rescue a deserving dog. While this may help to distract you from your grieving process, this is not really fair to the new fur member of your family.

Bringing a new pet into a home that is depressed and grieving the loss of a long time canine member may create behavioural problems for the new dog, who will be faced with learning all about their new home while also dealing with the unstable energy of the grieving family.

A better scenario would be to allow yourself the time to properly grieve by waiting a minimum of one month to allow yourself and your family to feel happier and more stable before deciding upon sharing your home with another dog.

The grieving process will be different for everyone and you will know when the time is right to consider sharing your home with another canine companion.

6. The Rainbow Bridge Poem

"Just this side of heaven
is a place called Rainbow Bridge.

When an animal dies that has been
especially close to someone here,
that pet goes to Rainbow Bridge.
There are meadows and hills for all of our special friends
so they can run and play together.
There is plenty of food, water and sunshine,
and our friends are warm and comfortable.

All the animals who had been ill and old
are restored to health and vigor;
those who were hurt or maimed
are made whole and strong again,
just as we remember them in our dreams
of days and times gone by.
The animals are happy and content,
except for one small thing;
they each miss someone very special to them,
who had to be left behind.

They all run and play together,
but the day comes when one suddenly stops
and looks into the distance.
His bright eyes are intent; His eager body quivers.
Suddenly he begins to run from the group,
flying over the green grass,
his legs carrying him faster and faster.

You have been spotted,
and when you and your special friend finally meet,
you cling together in joyous reunion,
never to be parted again.

197

The happy kisses rain upon your face;
your hands again caress the beloved head,
and you look once more into the trusting eyes
of your pet, so long gone from your life
but never absent from your heart.

Then you cross Rainbow Bridge together...."

- Author unknown

7. Memorials

There are as many unique ways to honour the passing of a beloved pet, as each of our fur friends is unique and special to us.

For instance, you may wish to have your fur friend cremated and preserve their ashes in a special urn or sprinkle their ashes along their favourite walk.

Perhaps you will want to have a special marker, photo bereavement, photo engraved Rainbow Bridge Poem, or wooden plaque created in honour of your lost friend.

You may wish to keep their memory close to you at all times by having a DNA remembrance pendant or bracelet designed.

As well, there are support groups, such as Rainbow Bridge, which is a grief support community, to help you and your family through this painful period of loss and grief.

Chapter 14) Cavachons, the law, insurance and micro chipping

Microchip your dog. You need to be contactable if your dog wanders off. If he or she goes missing and is injured and the RSPCA or the pound can't find an owner it will be put down. It is policy to put down injured strays. Even if your dog isn't injured, just a bit old and maybe deaf with a bit of a limp – this can be seen as a sign of brain damage and with no chip there will be no way of finding out the truth. My neighbour's elderly dog, Lilly, was a lovely little thing. A 17 year old Parson's Rustle, who was going blind in both eyes and her arthritis made her walk stiffly. When she escaped through the cat flap it was believed that she had been hit by a car. She was put down because there was no way of finding her owners, or of knowing that she was so old.

The microchip contains your contact details, your dogs name, breed and age. This information can literally save your dog's life.

A chip is also useful if it ever comes to ownership disputes. Say your little dog is stolen and you see them 3 years later at a show? If they are micro chipped you can prove that it's your dog.

While you're not legally obliged to have your dog insured, you are obliged to take care of its physical wellbeing. And as you'll love your Cavachon before they even arrive, you'll want to provide the best standards of health care you can. Veterinary treatment can be very expensive and unless you have a couple of thousands in the bank for emergencies, it makes sense to have your dog insured, especially if they go outside. A broken dog's leg in the UK can cost over £1300 to treat and in the USA it can cost $3000. If your dog gets in a tangle with a car – and even the best trained dogs can decide they like to chase cars – and isn't insured, it could be a choice between keeping your car and getting your dog treated. Even lap dogs can have accidents, tripping over stairs or knocking heavy things onto themselves. Not having your dog insured simply isn't worth it.

The problem of choice comes when you have to decide what type of insurance you want.

Probably your best bet is to try one of the insurance comparison websites. This will give you a flavour of what you can expect to pay. You will need to key in details about yourself and your pet. Some sites will want your pet's date of birth, how much you paid for it, and its microchip number.

The insurance you'll be looking for is lifetime cover- this means that your insurer can't back out of insuring you when your dog gets old and its veterinary bills shoot up.

There are several considerations to be aware of before choosing to purchase a pet insurance policy, including:
Is your dog required to undergo a physical exam? Most insurers don't require this if you insure with them from puppyhood.

Is there a waiting period before the policy becomes active? Again, this isn't typical, but insurance companies have to cover themselves from people buying insurance.

What percentage of the bill does the insurance company pay after the deductible? You want to know that they pay enough of the bill for you to be able to afford any extras out of the blue.

Are payments limited or capped in any way? A lot of insurers will have limits on how much they will pay per injury or sickness and have different limits for different types of problems.

Does the plan cover pre-existing conditions?
Some do, but these are rare and more expensive.

Does the plan cover chronic or reoccurring medical problems? There are more and more insurance companies that cover chronic or reoccurring problems. This is why you need to speak to a person when you buy insurance – phone the insurance companies and ask. Keep notes of what you are told.

Can you choose any vet or animal hospital to treat your pet? Most insurance companies will let you decide where your pet will be treated.

Are prescription medications covered? Again, most insurers now cover medications, but this will depend on what your excess is.

Are you covered when travelling with your pet? It's a good idea to phone your insurer to make sure you are covered before you go anywhere.

Does the policy pay if your pet is being treated and then dies? Again, most companies cover this, but you should check when you buy your policy.

Licensing

Many cities and jurisdictions around the world require that dogs be licensed.
Usually a dog license is an identifying tag that the dog will be required to wear on their collar. The tag will have an identifying number and a contact number for the registering organization, so that if someone finds a lost dog wearing a tag, the owner of the dog can be contacted.
Most dogs' tags are only valid for one year, and will need to be renewed annually at the beginning of every New Year, which involves paying a fee that can vary from jurisdiction to jurisdiction.

For instance, owners of dogs living in Beijing, China must pay a licensing fee of $600 (£360), while licensing for dogs living in Great Britain was abolished in 1987.

Ireland and Northern Ireland both require dogs to be licensed and in Germany dog ownership is taxed, rather than requiring licensing, with higher taxes being paid for breeds of dogs deemed to be "dangerous" (Cavachons aren't seen as dangerous).

Most US states and municipalities have licensing laws in effect and Canadian, Australian and New Zealand dogs also must be licensed, with the yearly cost approximately $30 to $50 (£18 to £30) depending upon whether the dog is spayed or neutered.

UK

Under UK law you are responsible for the health and wellbeing of your animal. You are responsible for the nutritional needs of your animal.

It is an offence not to provide adequate food and water.

It is an offence not to provide access to shelter.

It is an offence to allow your animal to live in unclean conditions.

It is an offence to go away without making provisions for the care of an animal.

It is an offence to intentionally harm an animal or to knowingly allow an animal to come to harm.

It is an offence not to provide adequate veterinary care.

If you are having financial difficulties this is no excuse, but the RSPCA and PDSA may be able to help out.

USA

According to the animal welfare act of 1996, owners have legal responsibilities to their animals.

It is an offence to allow an animal to remain in pain.

It is an offence to deny, purposefully or by omission, access to adequate food and water.

It is an offence to cause pain or distress or allow pain or distress to be caused.

You must comply with humane end points. (Humane endpoints are chosen to minimize or terminate the pain or distress of the experimental animals via euthanasia rather than waiting for their deaths as the endpoint.)

Forums and information

Dog training websites

http://www.cesarsway.com

http://www.cavachoncove.com/

Websites for finding puppies

UK

http://www.preloved.co.uk

http://www.pets4homes.co.uk

http://www.cavachons.co.uk

USA

http://www.4everpuppies.com

http://www.puppyfind.com/cavachon.php

http://www.greenfieldpuppies.com

Published by IMB Publishing 2014